D0769763

THE RESILIENT SECTOR

THE FOUNDATION CENTER
312 SUTTER ST., #312
SAN FRANCISCO, CA 94108

AUG 2 4 2004

FOUNDATION CENTER

00007011

602
SAL
STA
RES

THE RESILIENT SECTOR

THE STATE OF NONPROFIT AMERICA

LESTER M. SALAMON

THE FOUNDATION CENTER
312 SUTTER ST., #312
SAN FRANCISCO CA 94108

AUG 2 4 2004

BROOKINGS INSTITUTION PRESS
Washington, D.C.

Published in collaboration with the Aspen Institute

ABOUT BROOKINGS

The Brookings Institution is a private nonprofit organization devoted to research, education, and publication on important issues of domestic and foreign policy. Its principal purpose is to bring knowledge to bear on current and emerging policy problems. The Institution maintains a position of neutrality on issues of public policy. Interpretations or conclusions in Brookings publications should be understood to be solely those of the authors.

ABOUT ASPEN

Founded in 1950, the Aspen Institute is a global forum for leveraging the power of leaders to improve the human condition. Through its seminar and policy programs, the Institute fosters enlightened, morally responsible leadership and convenes leaders and policymakers to address the foremost challenges of the new century.

Copyright © 2003
Lester M. Salamon

All rights reserved. No part of this publication may be reproduced or transmitted in any form or by any means without permission in writing from the Brookings Institution Press, 1775 Massachusetts Avenue, N.W., Washington, D.C. 20036 (fax: 202/797-6195 or e-mail: permissions@brookings.edu).

Library of Congress Cataloging-in-Publication data
Salamon, Lester M.
    The resilient sector : the state of nonprofit America / Lester M.
Salamon.
    p.   cm.
Includes bibliographical references and index.
    ISBN 0-8157-7679-9 (alk. paper)
    1. Nonprofit organizations—United States. I. Title.
    HD2769.2.U6S246 2003
    338.7'4—dc21   2003013019

9 8 7 6 5 4 3 2 1

The paper used in this publication meets minimum requirements of the American National Standard for Information Sciences—Permanence of Paper for Printed Library Materials: ANSI Z39.48-1992.

Typeset in Adobe Garamond

Composition by Cynthia Stock,
Silver Spring, Maryland

Printed by R. R. Donnelley
Harrisonburg, Virginia

Contents

THE RESILIENT SECTOR

1

Introduction

When three hijacked planes crashed into the World Trade Center and the Pentagon on the morning of September 11, 2001, the police, fire, and military organs of New York City, Washington, D.C., and the U.S. government were not the only entities to respond with heroism and *élan*. The events of that horrific morning also triggered a spirited response from that vast, uncharted network of private voluntary institutions that forms the unseen social infrastructure of American life. In small towns and large metropolises, from Seattle to Savannah, people rushed forward to offer assistance. In part, the responses were spontaneous and unstructured. But in far larger part they were organized and orchestrated, mobilized by the vast assortment of organizations and institutions that constitute what is increasingly recognized as a distinct, if not wholly understood, sector of our national life known variously as the "nonprofit," the "charitable," or the "civil society" sector.

Like the arteries of a living organism, these organizations carry a life force that has long been a centerpiece of American culture—a faith in the capacity of individual action to improve the quality of human life. They thus embody two seemingly contradictory impulses that form the heart of American character: a deep-seated commitment to freedom and individual initiative and an equally fundamental realization that people live in communities and that they consequently have responsibilities that extend beyond themselves. Uniquely among American institutions, those in the nonprofit sector blend these competing impulses, creating a special class of entities dedicated to mobilizing *private initiative for the common good.*

The terrorists who crashed civilian jetliners into unarmed buildings on that fine September morning did not, therefore, assault a nation without the capacity to respond. But that capacity extended well beyond the conventional and visible institutions of government. It embraced as well a largely invisible social infrastructure of private, charitable groups and the supportive impulses to volunteer and give that it has helped to nurture.

And respond it did. Within two months, individuals, corporations, and foundations had contributed $1.3 billion in assistance to a wide array of relief efforts. Blood donations alone were estimated to have increased between 250,000 and 400,000 pints in the wake of the disaster.[1] Some of the institutions involved in mobilizing this response were household words—the Red Cross, the Salvation Army, United Way. Others were established but less well-known institutions, like the New York Community Trust, the Community Service Society of New York, and the Chicago Mercantile Exchange Foundation. And still others were created especially to deal with this crisis—the September 11 Fund, the Twin Towers Fund, Trial Lawyers Care (to assist victims with legal issues), and the Alaska Culinary Association (to benefit families of restaurant workers killed in the World Trade Center collapse). Altogether, some 200 charitable organizations reportedly pitched in to help directly with the relief and recovery effort in New York alone, and countless others were involved more indirectly. According to one survey, an astounding 70 percent of all Americans made some kind of contribution to this response.[2]

Revealing though this episode was of the remarkable strengths of America's "third," or nonprofit, sector, however, it simultaneously revealed the sector's limitations as well. Private voluntary groups, though highly effective in mobilizing individuals to act, are far less well equipped to structure the resulting activity. In short order, therefore, the fragile systems of nonprofit response were severely challenged by the enormity of the crisis they confronted in the aftermath of September 11. Individual agencies, concerned about their autonomy, resisted efforts to coordinate their responses, either with each other or with governmental authorities. Individuals in need of assistance consequently found it necessary to navigate a multitude of separate agencies, each with its own eligibility criteria and targeted forms of aid. Inevitably, delays and inequities occurred; many individuals fell through the slats, while others benefited from multiple sources of assistance. What is more, misunderstandings arose between the donors, most of whom apparently intended their contributions to be used for immediate relief, and some agencies, most notably the Red Cross, which hoped to squirrel at least some of the contributions away for longer-term recovery, general institutional support, and other, less visible, disasters down the road. What began as an inspiring demonstration of the power of America's charitable community thus quickly became a demonstration of the sector's limitations as well.[3]

In this, the story of the nonprofit sector's response to the crisis of September 11 is emblematic of its position in American life more generally. Long celebrated as a fundamental part of the American heritage, America's nonprofit organizations have long suffered from structural shortcomings that limit the role they can play. This juxtaposition of strengths and limitations, in turn, has fueled a lively ideological contest over the extent to which we should rely on these institutions to handle critical public needs, with conservatives focusing laser-like on the sector's strengths and liberals often restricting their attention to its weaknesses instead. Through it all, though largely unheralded and perhaps unrecognized by either side, a classically American compromise has taken shape. This compromise was forged early in the nation's history, but it was broadened and solidified in the 1960s. Under it, nonprofit organizations in an ever-widening range of fields were made the beneficiaries of government support to provide a growing array of services—from health care to scientific research—that Americans wanted but were reluctant to have government directly provide.[4] More than any other single factor, this government-nonprofit partnership is responsible for the growth of the nonprofit sector as we know it today.

Beginning in the early 1980s, however, that compromise came under considerable assault. At the same time, the country's nonprofit institutions have faced an extraordinary range of other challenges as well—significant demographic shifts, fundamental changes in public policy and public attitudes, new commercial impulses, growing competition from for-profit providers, shifts in the basic structure of key industries in which nonprofits are involved, massive technological developments, and changes in life-style, to cite just a few. Although nonprofit America has responded with creativity to many of these challenges, the responses have pulled it in directions that are, at best, not well understood, and at worst, corrosive of the sector's special character and role.

Despite the significance of these developments, however, little headway has been made in tracking them in a timely and systematic way, in assessing the impact they are having both generally and for particular types of organizations, and in getting the results into the hands of nonprofit practitioners, policymakers, the press, and the public at large. This book is intended to fill this gap, to offer a clear, up-to-date assessment of a set of institutions that we have long taken for granted but that the Frenchman Alexis de Toqueville recognized nearly 170 years ago to be "more deserving of our attention" than any other part of the American experiment.[5] More specifically, the book makes available in a more accessible form the summary of a much larger inquiry into the state of America's nonprofit sector that the present author carried out with an extraordinary team of collaborators and that was published in a prior volume.[6]

The basic story that emerged from this larger project, and that is the theme of this book, is fundamentally a story of *resilience*, of a set of institutions and traditions facing enormous challenges and also important opportunities, but that has found ways to respond to both, often with considerable creativity and resolve. Indeed, nonprofit America appears to be well along in a fundamental process of "re-engineering" that calls to mind the similar process that large segments of America's business sector have undergone since the late 1980s.[7] Faced with an increasingly competitive and changing environment, nonprofit organizations and the institutions and traditions that support them have been called on to make fundamental changes in the way they operate. And that is just what they have been doing.

What is involved here, moreover, is not simply the importation of "business methods" into nonprofit organizations, though that is sometimes how it is portrayed.[8] While nonprofits are becoming more "market oriented" and "businesslike," the business methods they are adopting have themselves undergone fundamental change in recent years, and many of the changes have involved incorporating management approaches that have long been associated with nonprofit work—such as the critical importance of mission to organizational success, the ethos of service to clients as a cornerstone of organizational purpose, and the need to imbue staff with a sense of purpose that goes beyond the narrow concept of maximizing profits. In a sense, these long-time nonprofit management principles have now been fused with business-management techniques to produce a blended body of management concepts that is penetrating business and nonprofit management alike.

Like all processes of change, this one is far from even. What is more, it is not without its costs, both for individual organizations and for the nonprofit sector as a whole. Some organizations have thus been swept up in the winds of change, while others have hardly felt a breeze, or having felt it, have not been in a position to respond. What is more, it is far from clear which group has made the right decision or left the sector as a whole better off, since the consequences of some of the changes are far from certain, and at any rate are mixed.

Any account of the state of nonprofit America must therefore be a story in three parts, focusing, first, on the challenges and opportunities that America's nonprofit sector is confronting, then examining how the sector's institutions are responding to these challenges and opportunities, and finally assessing the consequences of these responses both for individual organizations and subsectors and for nonprofit America as a whole. Against this backdrop, it will then be possible to identify some of the steps that are needed to allow America's nonprofit institutions to continue to make the contributions of which they are capable.

The balance of this volume offers such an account. To set the stage for it, however, it may be useful to explain more fully what the nonprofit sector is and why it deserves our attention.

2

The Stakes:
The Nonprofit Sector
and Why We Need It

If the nonprofit sector is one of the most important components of American life, it is also one of the least understood. Few people are even aware of this sector's existence, though most have some direct contact with it at some point in their lives. Included within this sector is a vast assortment of organizations: the nation's religious congregations, its labor unions and professional associations, its social clubs, most of its premier hospitals and universities, almost all of its orchestras and opera companies, a significant share of its theaters, the bulk of its environmental advocacy and civil rights organizations, and huge numbers of its family service, children's service, neighborhood development, antipoverty, and community health facilities. Also included are the numerous support organizations, such as foundations and community chests, that help to generate financial assistance for these organizations, as well as the traditions of giving, volunteering, and service they help to foster.

More formally, the nonprofit sector consists of private organizations that are prohibited from distributing any profits they may generate to those who control or support them. These organizations are generally exempted from federal, and often from state and local, taxation on grounds that they serve some public purpose. Hence they are often referred to as "tax-exempt" organizations. But the range of purposes for which such tax exemption is granted is quite broad. Federal tax law, for example, identifies no fewer than twenty-six classes of such organizations, ranging from political parties to cemetery companies.[1]

For our purposes here, I focus on the largest, and most visible, sub-set of these organizations: those that are eligible for exemption from federal income taxation under section 501(c)(3) of the tax code, plus the closely related "social welfare organizations" eligible for exemption under section 501(c)(4) of this code. Included here are organizations that operate "exclusively for religious, charitable, scientific, or educational purposes" and that do not distribute any profits they may generate to any private shareholder or individual. Alone among tax-exempt organizations, the 501(c)(3) organizations are also eligible to receive tax deductible contributions from individuals and businesses, a reflection of the fact that they are expected to serve broad public purposes, as opposed to the interests and needs of the members of the organizations alone.[2]

Scale

No one knows for sure how many such nonprofit organizations exist in the United States, since large portions of the sector are essentially unincorporated and the data available on even the formal organizations are notoriously incomplete. A conservative estimate would put the number of formally constituted 501(c)(3) and 501(c)(4) organizations at 1.2 million as of the mid-1990s, including an estimated 350,000 churches and other religious congregations.[3] As of 1998, these organizations employed close to 11 million paid workers, or over 7 percent of the U.S. work force, and enlisted the equivalent of another 5.7 million full-time employees as volunteers.[4] This means

Figure 2-1. *Nonprofit Employment in Relation to Employment*
in Major U.S. Industries, 1998

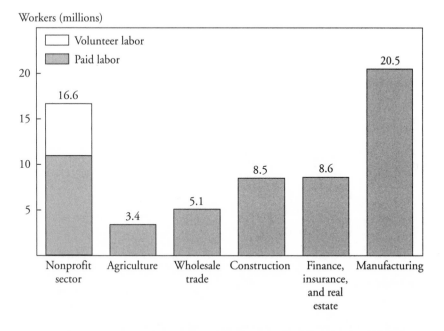

Workers (millions)

Source: Murray S. Weitzman and others, *The New Nonprofit Almanac and Desk Reference*
(San Francisco: Jossey-Bass, 2002), pp. 33, 23, 80; U.S. Census Bureau, *Statistical Abstract of
the United States,* 120th ed. (Government Printing Office, 2000), p. 420.

that the paid employment alone in nonprofit organizations is three
times that in agriculture, twice that in wholesale trade, and nearly 50
percent greater than that in construction and in finance, insurance,
and real estate, as shown in figure 2-1. With volunteer labor included,
employment in the nonprofit sector, at 16.6 million, approaches that
in all branches of manufacturing combined (20.5 million).[5]

Most of this nonprofit employment is concentrated in three
fields—health (43 percent), education (22 percent), and social services
such as day care, foster care, and family counseling (18 percent). With
volunteers included, the distribution of employment changes significantly, with the religious share swelling to 23 percent and health drop-
ping to 34 percent (figure 2-2)

Figure 2-2. *Distribution of Nonprofit Employment, Paid and Volunteer,
by Field, 1998*[a]

Percent of total

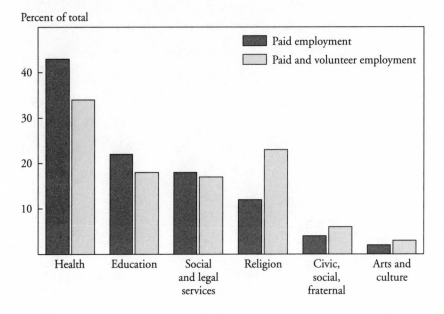

Source: Author's estimates based on data in Weitzman and others, *The Nonprofit Almanac
and Desk Reference;* Virginia B. Hodgkinson and Murray S. Weitzman, *Nonprofit Almanac: 1996/97*
(San Francisco: Jossey-Bass, 1996).
    a. Paid employment, n = 10.9 million. Paid and volunteer employment, n = 16.6 million.

These large categories disguise, however, the huge array of separate
services and activities in which nonprofit organizations are involved. A
classification system developed by the National Center for Charitable
Statistics, for example, identifies no fewer than twenty-six major fields
of nonprofit activity, and sixteen functions—from accreditation to
fund-raising—in each. Each of the major fields is then further subdi-
vided into separate subfields. Thus, for example, the field of arts, culture, and humanities has fifty-six subfields; and the field of education
has forty-one. Altogether, this translates into several thousand poten-
tial types of nonprofit organizations.[6]

Even this fails to do justice to the considerable diversity of the
nonprofit sector. Most of the employment and economic resources of

this sector are concentrated in a relatively limited number of large organizations. However, most of the organizations are quite small, with few or no full-time employees. Of the nearly 670,000 organizations recorded on the Internal Revenue Service's list of formally registered 501(c)(3) organizations (exclusive of religious congregations and foundations) as of 1998, for example, only about a third, or 224,000, filed the information form (Form 990) required of all organizations with expenditures of $25,000 or more. The remaining two-thirds of the organizations are thus either inactive or below the $25,000 spending threshold for filing.[7] Even among the filers, moreover, the top 4 percent accounted for nearly 70 percent of the reported expenditures, while the bottom 40 percent accounted for less than 1 percent of the total.[8]

Roles and Functions

Quite apart from their economic importance, nonprofit organizations make crucial contributions to national and community life.[9]

The Service Role

In the first place, nonprofit organizations are *service providers*: they deliver much of the hospital care, higher education, social services, cultural entertainment, employment and training, low-income housing, community development, and emergency aid services available in the United States. More concretely, this set of organizations constitutes:

—half of the nation's hospitals;

—one-third of its health clinics;

—over a quarter of its nursing homes;

—nearly half (46 percent) of its higher education institutions;

—four-fifths (80 percent) of its individual and family service agencies;

—70 percent of its vocational rehabilitation facilities;

—30 percent of its day care centers;

—over 90 percent of its orchestras and operas; and

—the delivery vehicles for 70 percent of its foreign disaster assistance.

While disagreements exist over how "distinctive" nonprofit services are compared to those provided by businesses or governments, non-profits are well known for identifying and responding to unmet needs, for innovating, and for delivering services of exceptional quality. Non-profit organizations thus pioneered assistance to AIDS victims, hos-pice care, emergency shelter for the homeless, food pantries for the hungry, drug abuse treatment efforts, and dozens more, too numerous to mention. Similarly, many of the nation's premier cultural and edu-cational institutions are private, nonprofit organizations—institutions like Harvard, Princeton, Yale, Stanford, the University of Chicago, Johns Hopkins University, the Metropolitan Museum of Art, and the Cleveland Symphony, to name just a few. While public and for-profit organizations also provide crucial services, there is no denying the extra dimension added by the country's thousands of private, non-profit groups in meeting public needs that neither the market nor the state can, or will, adequately address.

The Advocacy Role

In addition to delivering services, nonprofit organizations also con-tribute to national life by identifying unaddressed problems and bringing them to public attention, by protecting basic human rights, and by giving voice to a wide assortment of social, political, environ-mental, ethnic, and community interests and concerns. Most of the social movements that have animated American life over the past cen-tury or more operated in and through the nonprofit sector. Included here are the antislavery, women's suffrage, populist, progressive, civil rights, environmental, antiwar, women's, gay rights, and conservative movements. The nonprofit sector has thus helped make the constitu-tional protections of free speech operational by permitting individuals to join their voices with others to effect social and political change. As such, it has operated as a critical social safety valve, permitting aggrieved groups to bring their concerns to broader public attention and to rally support to improve their circumstances. This advocacy role may, in fact, be more important to the nation's social health than are the service functions this sector also performs.

The Expressive Role

Political and policy concerns are not the only ones to which the non-profit sector gives expression. Rather, this set of institutions provides the vehicles through which an enormous variety of other sentiments and impulses—artistic, religious, cultural, ethnic, social, recreational—also find expression. Opera companies, symphonies, soccer clubs, churches, synagogues, fraternal societies, book clubs, and girl scouts are just some of the manifestations of this expressive function. Through them, nonprofit organizations enrich human existence and contribute to the social and cultural vitality of national and community life.

The Community-Building Role

Nonprofit organizations are also important in building what scholars are increasingly coming to call "social capital," those bonds of trust and reciprocity that seem to be crucial for a democratic polity and a market economy to function effectively.[10] Alexis de Tocqueville understood this point well when he wrote in *Democracy in America* that:

> Feelings and opinions are recruited, the heart is enlarged, and the human mind is developed, only by the reciprocal influence of men upon one another . . . these influences are almost null in democratic countries; they must therefore be artificially created and this can only be accomplished by associations.[11]

By establishing connections among individuals, involvement in associations teaches norms of cooperation that carry over into political and economic life, enlarging the nation's pool of social capital.

The Value Guardian Role

Finally, nonprofit organizations embody, and therefore help to nurture and sustain, a crucial national value emphasizing individual initiative in the public good.[12] They thus give institutional expression to two seemingly contradictory principles that are both important parts of American national character—the principle of *individualism*, the notion that people should have the freedom to act on matters that concern them; and the principle of *solidarity*, the notion the people have responsibilities not only to themselves, but to their fellow human beings and to the communities of which they are part. By fusing these two principles, nonprofit organizations reinforce both, establishing an arena of action through which individuals can take the initiative not simply to promote their own well-being but also to advance the well-being of others. This is not simply an abstract function, moreover. It takes tangible form in the more than $200 billion in private charitable gifts that nonprofit organizations help to generate from the American public annually and in the 15.8 billion hours of volunteer time they stimulate for a diverse array of purposes.

In short, nonprofit America is not only a sizable part of the American economy. It remains, as well, a crucial contributor to the quality of American life.

3

The Challenges

Despite the important contributions it makes, nonprofit America has found itself in a time of testing in recent years. To be sure, it is not alone in this. For-profit corporations and governments have also experienced enormous challenges over the past twenty years. But the challenges facing nonprofit organizations are especially daunting, since they go to the heart of this sector's operations and raise questions about its very existence.

More specifically, nonprofit America has confronted six critical challenges over the recent past. From all indications, moreover, these challenge seem likely to persist, and in some cases to intensify, in the years ahead. In this chapter, I examine these challenges before turning in subsequent chapters to the opportunities America's nonprofits have also had available to them, and to the way they have responded to both.

The Fiscal Challenge

Perhaps the most fundamental challenge America's nonprofit organizations have experienced in the recent past has been a significant fiscal squeeze. To be sure, fiscal distress has been a way of life for this sector throughout its history. But this eased significantly in the aftermath of World War II, and even more so in the 1960s, when the federal government expanded its funding, first, of scientific research, and then, of a wide range of health and social services. What is not widely recognized is that the government efforts to stimulate science and overcome poverty and ill health during this period relied heavily on nonprofit organizations for their operation, following a pattern that had been established early in our nation's history.[1] By the late 1970s, as a consequence, federal support to American nonprofit organizations outdistanced private charitable support by a factor of 2 to 1, and state and local governments provided additional aid. What is more, this support percolated through a wide swath of the nonprofit sector, providing needed financial nourishment to colleges, universities, hospitals, health clinics, day care centers, nursing homes, residential treatment facilities, employment and training centers, family service agencies, drug abuse prevention programs, and many more. Indeed, much of the modern nonprofit sector as we know it took shape during this period as a direct outgrowth of expanded government support.

Federal Retrenchment

This widespread pattern of government support to nonprofit organizations suffered a severe shock, however, in the early 1980s. Committed to a policy of fiscal restraint and seemingly unaware of the extent to which public resources were underwriting private, nonprofit action, the Reagan administration launched a significant assault on federal spending in precisely the areas where federal support to nonprofit organizations was most extensive—social and human services, education and training, community development, and nonhospital health services. Although the budget cuts that occurred during this period were nowhere near as severe as originally proposed, federal support to nonprofit organizations, outside of Medicare and Medicaid (the large federal health finance programs), declined by approximately 25 percent in real dollar terms in the early 1980s and did not return to its 1980 level until the latter 1990s.[2] Although some state governments boosted their own spending in many of these fields, the increases were not sufficient to offset the federal reductions. Indeed, outside of pensions, public education, and health, overall government social welfare spending declined by more than $30 billion between 1981 and 1989. Nonprofit organizations in the fields of community development, employment and training, social services, and community health were particularly hard hit by these reductions.

Although these fiscal pressures eased significantly during the 1990s, as a booming economy and a series of policy shifts permitted an expansion of the government support available to nonprofit organizations, the experience of the 1980s and early 1990s left a lingering fiscal scar. That scar was re-opened in the early years of the new century by a combination of tax reductions, economic recession, and increased military and antiterror spending that is causing new cutbacks in health, education, and social welfare spending, and therefore new pressures on nonprofit finances. After running unaccustomed surpluses in the late 1990s, the federal government thus registered a sizable deficit in fiscal year 2002 and appears headed for escalating deficits in the years beyond. To cope with the shortfall, new pressures are being put on the discretionary spending programs so important to nonprofit finance.[3] What is more, state governments are facing even more severe fiscal constraints. All but seven states experienced budget shortfalls in 2002, and the prospects for subsequent years are even more dire, producing what one observer called "the worst state financial landscape since at least World War II.[4]

Changing Forms of Public Support

Not just the amount, but also the form, of government support to the nonprofit sector changed during this period, moreover. Where previously government relied heavily on grants and contracts and gave nonprofits the inside track, during the 1980s and 1990s government

program managers were encouraged to promote for-profit involvement in government contract work, including that for human services.[5] More significantly, the use of grants and contracts itself gave way
increasingly to forms of assistance, such as vouchers and tax expenditures, that channel aid to the consumers of services rather than the
producers, thus requiring nonprofits to compete for clients in the market, where for-profits have traditionally had the edge.[6] Already by
1980, the majority (53 percent) of federal assistance to nonprofit
organizations took the form of such consumer subsidies, much of it
through the Medicare and Medicaid programs.[7] By 1986, this stood at
70 percent, and it continued to rise into the 1990s.[8]

In part, this shift toward consumer subsidies resulted from the con-
centration of the budget cuts of the 1980s on the so-called discretionary spending programs, which tended to be producer-side grant
and contract programs, while Medicare and Medicaid—both of them
consumer-side subsidies—continued to grow.[9] In part also, however,
the shift toward consumer-side subsidies reflects the ascendance of
conservative political forces that favor forms of assistance that maxi-
mized consumer choice in the marketplace. The price of securing conservative support for new or expanded programs of relevance to nonprofit organizations in the late 1980s and early 1990s, therefore, was
to structure them as vouchers or tax expenditures. The new Child
Care and Development Block Grant enacted in 1990 and then reau-
thorized and expanded as part of the welfare reform legislation in
1996, for example, specifically gave states the option to use the $5 bil-
lion in federal funds provided for day care to finance voucher payments to eligible families rather than grants or contracts to day care
providers, and most states exercised this option. As of 1998, therefore,
well over 80 percent of the children receiving day care assistance under
this program were receiving it through such voucher certificates, while
an additional $2 billion in federal day care subsidies were delivered
through a special child care tax credit.[10] Nearly $7 billion were thus
provided in new consumer-side day care subsidies, much more than

the $2.8 billion allocated for producer-side subsidies to social service providers under the federal government's Social Services Block Grant, long the major source of government funding for day care and other social services.[11] Nonprofit day care providers, like their counterparts in other fields, were thus thrown increasingly into the private market to secure even public funding for their activities. In the process, they were obliged to master complex billing and reimbursement systems and to learn how to "market" their services to potential "customers." What is more, the reimbursement rates in many of these programs have often failed to cover the full costs of the service, putting a further squeeze on nonprofit budgets and making it harder to sustain mission-critical functions such as advocacy and charity care.[12]

Not only did government support to nonprofit organizations change its form during this period, but so did important elements of private support. The most notable development here was the emergence of "managed care" in the health field, displacing the traditional pattern of fee-for-service medicine. Medicare provided an important impetus for this development by replacing its cost-based reimbursement system for hospitals in the early 1980s with a system of fixed payments for particular procedures. Corporations, too, responded to the rapid escalation of health care benefits for their workers by moving aggressively during the 1980s to replace standard fee-for-service insurance plans with managed care plans that featured up-front "capitation" payments to managed care providers. These providers then inserted themselves between patients and health care providers, negotiating rates with the providers and deciding which procedures were truly necessary. By 1997, close to 75 percent of the employees in medium and large establishments, and 62 percent of the employees in small establishments, were covered by some type of managed care plan.[13] More recently, managed care has expanded into the social services field, subjecting nonprofit drug treatment, rehabilitation service, and mental health treatment facilities to the same competitive pressures and reimbursement limits as hospitals have been confronting.

Table 3-1. *Individual Giving as a Share of Personal Income*

Period	Giving as a percent of personal income
1970–74	1.89
1975–79	1.77
1980–84	1.75
1985–89	1.69
1990–97	1.64
1998–2000	1.89
2001	1.85

Source: Private giving from AAFRC Trust for Philanthropy, *Giving USA 2002* (Indianapolis, 2002), p. 169; personal income data from *Survey of Current Business* (August 2002), p. 139.

Tepid Growth of Private Giving

Adding to the fiscal pressure nonprofits have been facing has been the continued inability of private philanthropy to offset cutbacks in government support and finance expanded nonprofit responses to community needs. To be sure, private giving has grown considerably over the recent past. Between 1977 and 1997, for example, total private giving grew by some 90 percent after adjusting for inflation, roughly equivalent to the growth of gross domestic product. However, this lumps the amounts provided for the actual operations of charities in a given year with large endowment gifts to foundations, universities, and other institutions, which typically are not available for immediate use, as well as with gifts to religious congregations, most of which go to the upkeep of the congregations and clergy.[14] When we focus on the private gifts available to support nonprofit human service, arts, education, health, and advocacy organizations in a given year, the growth rate was closer to 62 percent, still impressive but well below the 81 percent growth rate of gross domestic product.[15] Indeed, as a share of personal income, private giving has been declining steadily in the United States: from an average of 1.89 percent in the early 1970s down to 1.75 percent in the early 1980s and to 1.64 percent in the early to mid-1990s (see table 3-1). Especially distressing has been the disappointing rate of giving by the well-off, which has fallen considerably as

Table 3-2. *Recent Trends in Nonprofit Revenue from Philanthropy,
1977 and 1997*[a]

| | Percent of nonprofit revenue from philanthropy | |
Type of organization	1977	1997
All nonprofits	27	20
Excluding religious	18	12

Source: Author's calculations from data in Murray S. Weitzman and others, *The New Nonprofit Almanac and Desk Reference* (San Francisco: Jossey-Bass, 2002), pp. 96–97.

a. Includes individual giving and foundation and corporate support.

a share of their income over the past decade or more, perhaps as a result of tax rate changes that lowered the tax rates on the wealthy, and hence their financial incentives to give.[16] While giving as a share of personal income increased somewhat in the boom times of the late 1990s, it barely returned to its 1970s level; and the stock market sell-off and recession of 2000–02 have constrained its further growth, despite the outpouring of support in response to the September 11 events.[17] Indeed, after adjusting for inflation, private giving actually declined in 2001, even with the September 11 boost.[18]

Although giving has grown in absolute terms, therefore, it has actually lost ground as a share of total income, falling from 18 percent of the total outside of religion in 1977 to 12 percent in 1997 (see table 3-2).[19] What is more, there is little evidence that this has substantially changed in more recent years. Indeed, many nonprofit organizations fear that September 11 may reduce their charitable receipts further, as resources are shifted to postdisaster relief and recovery.

The Competition Challenge

In addition to a fiscal challenge, nonprofit America has also faced a serious competitive challenge as a result of the striking growth of for-profit involvement in many traditional fields of nonprofit activity, from health care and welfare assistance to higher education and employment training. This, too, is not a wholly new development.

Table 3-3. *Nonprofit and For-Profit Roles in Selected Fields, 1982 and 1997*

	Percentage nonprofit		Percentage change in relative
Field	1982	1997	nonprofit share
Employment			
Child day care	52	38	−27
Job training	93	89	−4
Individual and family services	94	91	−3
Home health	60	28	−53
Kidney dialysis centers	22	15	−32
Facilities, participation			
Dialysis centers	58[a]	32	−45
Rehabilitation hospitals	70[a]	36	−50
Home health agencies	64[a]	33	−48
Health maintenance organizations	65[a]	26	−60
Residential treatment facilities for children	87[b]	68	−22
Psychiatric hospitals	19[a]	16	−16
Hospices	89[c]	76	−15
Mental health clinics	64[b]	57	−11
Higher education enrollments	96	89	−7
Nursing homes	20[b]	28	40
Acute care hospitals	58[a]	59	2

Source: U.S. Census Bureau, *U.S. Economic Census* (1999), Bradford H. Gray and Mark Schlesinger, "Health," in Lester M. Salamon, ed., *The State of Nonprofit America* (Brookings, 2002), pp. 68–69; National Center for Education Statistics, *Digest of Education Statistics 2000* (U.S. Department of Education, 2000), pp. 202–03, 209.
  a. Figure is for 1985.
  b. Figure is for 1986.
  c. Figure is for 1992.

Nonprofit arts institutions have long confronted competition from for-profit leisure and entertainment organizations, and for-profits have held a commanding position in the nursing home field for four decades. But the scope of competition appears to have broadened considerably in recent years, and in an increasing range of fields, nonprofits have been losing "market share." Thus the nonprofit share of day care jobs dropped from 52 percent to 38 percent between 1982 and 1997, a decline of some 27 percent (see table 3-3). Similarly sharp declines in the relative nonprofit share occurred among rehabilitation hospitals, home health agencies, health maintenance organizations

(HMOs), kidney dialysis centers, mental health clinics, and hospices. In many of these fields the absolute number of nonprofit facilities continued to grow, but the for-profit growth outpaced it. And in at least one crucial field—acute care hospitals—while the nonprofit *share* increased slightly, a significant reduction occurred in the *absolute number* of nonprofit (as well as public) facilities, so that the for-profit share of the total increased even more.

The range of for-profit firms competing with nonprofits has grown increasingly broad, moreover. For example, the recent welfare reform legislation, which seeks to move large numbers of welfare recipients from welfare dependence to employment, attracted defense contractors like Lockheed-Martin into the social welfare field. What these firms offer is less knowledge of human services than information-processing technology and contract management skills gained from serving as master contractors on huge military system projects, precisely the skills needed to manage the subcontracting systems required to prepare welfare recipients for work. Under many of these new arrangements, in fact, nonprofit providers are finding themselves serving as subcontractors to for-profit firms hired by state or local governments to manage the welfare reform process. Even the sacrosanct field of charitable fund-raising has recently experienced a significant for-profit incursion in the form of financial service firms such as Fidelity and Merrill Lynch. The Fidelity Charitable Gift Fund, established in 1991, thus gives Fidelity investors the opportunity to establish "donor-advised funds" with the same institution that manages their other investments. By 2000, this fund had attracted more assets than the nation's largest community foundation and distributed three times as much in grants.[20]

The reasons for this striking pattern of for-profit success are by no means clear and vary from field to field. One contributing factor, clearly, is the shift in the forms of public funding mentioned earlier: with most of the available government support now taking the form of consumer-side subsidies, nonprofits are having to compete for it by attracting subsidized customers in the marketplace, where for-profit firms have a natural advantage. The rise of HMOs and other "third-party payment" methods has had a similar effect, since such organizations put a special premium on price rather than quality or community roots in choosing providers, thus minimizing the comparative advantages of nonprofits.[21] Technological developments have also given for-profit firms a strategic edge. This is so because technology puts a premium on access to capital, and nonprofits have an inherent difficulty in generating capital because their nonprofit status makes it impossible for them to enter the equity markets and sell shares. Nonprofits are therefore at a particular disadvantage in fields where rapid increases in demand or technological innovations necessitate increased capital expenditures. In the past, national policy has recognized this problem by providing special tax and other benefits to particular types of nonprofit institutions, such as hospitals and universities, but such policies have not been extended to other fields and, in some instances, have been phased out if they once did exist.[22]

The Effectiveness Challenge

One consequence of the increased competition nonprofits are facing has been to intensify the pressure on them to perform, and to demonstrate that performance. The result is a third challenge: the effectiveness challenge. As management expert William Ryan has written: "Nonprofits are now forced to reexamine their reasons for existing in light of a market that rewards discipline and performance and emphasizes organizational capacity rather than for-profit or nonprofit status and mission. Nonprofits have no choice but to reckon with these forces."[23] This runs counter to long-standing theories in the nonprofit field that have emphasized this sector's distinctive advantage precisely in fields where "information asymmetry" makes it difficult to demonstrate performance, and where "trust" is consequently needed instead. Because they are not organized to pursue profits, it was argued, nonprofits are more worthy of such trust and therefore more reliable providers in such difficult-to-measure fields.[24]

In the current climate, however, such theories have few remaining adherents, at least among those who control the sector's purse strings. Government managers, themselves under pressure to demonstrate results because of the recent Government Performance and Results Act, are increasingly pressing their nonprofit contractors to deliver measurable results, too. Not to be outdone, prominent philanthropic institutions have jumped onto the performance bandwagon. United Way of America, for example, thus launched a bold performance measurement system in the mid-1990s, complete with website, performance measurement manual, and video, in order to induce member agencies to require performance measurement as a condition of local funding. Numerous foundations have moved in a similar direction, increasing the emphasis on evaluation both of their grantees and of their own programming.[25] Sessions on outcome measurement have become standard fare at foundation meetings and a new foundation affinity group called Grantmakers for Effective Organizations (GEO) has even been formed. In addition, a new "venture philanthropy" model has been attracting increased attention, and numerous adherents.[26] The key to this model is an investment approach to grant making that calls on philanthropic organizations to make long-term investments in nonprofit organizations, to focus on the organization rather than individual programs, to take a more active hand in organizational governance and operations, and to insist on measurable results.

The resulting "accountability environment" in which nonprofits are having to operate will doubtless produce many positive results. But it also increases the pressures on hard-pressed nonprofit managers to demonstrate progress in ways that neither they nor anyone else may be able to accomplish, at least not without far greater resources than are currently available for the task. What is more, accountability expectations often fail to acknowledge the multiple stakeholders whose accountability demands nonprofits must accommodate. The risk is great, therefore, that the measures most readily at hand, or those most responsive to the market test, will substitute for those most germane to the problems being addressed. That, at any rate, is the lesson of public sector experience with performance measurement, where, as one observer has put it, "the measurable drives out the important."[27] The increased focus on price rather than quality or community benefit in third-party contracting with health providers certainly supports this observation.

The Technology Challenge

Pressures from for-profit competitors have also accelerated the demands on nonprofits to incorporate new technology into their operations. Indeed, technology has become one of the great wildcards in the evolution of the contemporary nonprofit sector, as it has of the contemporary for-profit and government sectors. Like the other challenges identified here, technology's impact is by no means wholly negative. For example, new information technology is increasing the capacity of nonprofits to advocate, reducing the costs of mobilizing constituents and connecting to policymakers and allies. This observation finds confirmation in Jeffrey Berry's careful analysis of the growing influence of citizen groups, which he attributes in important part to access to television news.[28] Technology is also opening new ways to tap charitable contributions. The September 11 tragedy may well have marked a turning point in this regard, since some 10 percent of the funds raised came via the Internet.[29]

Nonprofit education, health, and arts institutions are also benefiting from technological change. For example, the "sage on a stage" model of education is being replaced by a "distributed learning" model that opens education and learning across earlier boundaries of place, age, and time. Medical practice has already been transformed by new technology, but genetic engineering and the new field of bionics, linking biosciences with electronics, promises even more dramatic breakthroughs, making it possible to deliver medical services not only in one's home but in one's body, through the implantation of biosensors that can think and react.[30] Digitization is having a similar effect in the arts world.[31] Three on-site classical music websites are already in operation, providing live, streaming transmissions of orchestral concerts from around the world, and this is just the beginning. A project of the Mellon Foundation is digitizing the collections of hundreds of museums at a level of technical sophistication unmatched by anything even imagined before. With their vast collections of artistic material, nonprofit museums, art galleries, opera companies, and other cultural institutions sit on vast stockpiles of cultural raw material that is potentially available for exploitation in the new digital era, and many are taking advantage of the opportunities.

But enticing as the opportunities opened by technological change may be to the nation's nonprofit institutions, they pose equally enormous challenges. Most obvious, perhaps, are the financial challenges. As one recent study notes: "Information technologies are resource intensive. They entail significant purchase costs, require significant training and upkeep, and yet become obsolete quickly."[32] Because of the structural disadvantages nonprofits face in raising capital due to their inability to enter the equity markets, however, the massive intrusion of new technological requirements into their work puts them at a distinct disadvantage vis-à-vis their for-profit competitors. We have already seen the consequences of this in the HMO industry, where the lack of capital following the discontinuation of government funding led to the rapid loss of market share to for-profit firms, which were better able to capitalize the huge investments in information-processing equipment required to manage the large risk pools that make managed care viable. Similar pressures are now at work in the social services industry, where managed care is also taking root and where the complex systems required to move welfare recipients into work has given an edge to defense contractors in the welfare reform arena.

Not only does technology threaten to alter further the balance between nonprofits and for-profits, but it also threatens to alter the structure of the nonprofit sector itself, advantaging larger organizations over smaller ones. This is due in part to the heavy fixed costs of the new technology. Already, concerns about a "digital divide" are surfacing within the sector, as survey after survey reveals the unequal distribution of both hardware and the capacity to adapt the hardware to organizational missions.[33] Though initially stimulating competition by giving even small upstarts access to huge markets, information technology also creates "network effects" that accentuate the advantages of dominant players.[34] Significant concerns have thus surfaced that e-philanthropy will allow large, well-known national nonprofits to raid the donor bases of local United Ways and operating charities and that information technology more generally will give exceptional advantages to large agencies in the competition for business partners, government funding, and foundation grants.

But the challenges posed by technology go far beyond financial or competitive considerations. Also at stake are fundamental philosophical issues that go to the heart of the nonprofit sector's mission and modes of operation. As Margaret Wyszomirski shows, such issues have surfaced especially vividly in the arts arena, where the new technology raises fundamental questions of aesthetics, creative control, and intellectual property rights.[35] Similar dilemmas confront educational institutions that are tempted by the new technologies to "brand" their products and package them for mass consumption, but at the risk of alienating their professoriat, losing the immediacy of direct student-faculty contact, and giving precedence to the packaging of knowledge over its discovery.

How these technological dilemmas are resolved could well determine how the nonprofit sector evolves in the years ahead. Nonprofit America can no more ignore them than any other component of national life.

The Legitimacy Challenge

The moral and philosophical challenges that American nonprofit organizations are confronting at the present time involve more than new technology, however. Rather, a serious fault line seems to have opened in the foundation of public trust on which the entire edifice of the nonprofit sector rests. This may be due in part to the unrealistic expectations that the public has of these institutions, expectations that the charitable sector, ironically, counts on and encourages. Also at work, however, has been the strident indictment that conservative politicians and commentators have lodged against many nonprofit organizations over the past two decades. The central charge in this indictment is that nonprofit charitable organizations have become just another special interest, regularly conspiring with government bureaucrats to escalate public spending, and doing so not so much out of real conviction about the needs being served as out of a desire to feather their own nests. Heritage Foundation president Edward Feulner put this case especially sharply in 1996, criticizing charities for urging Congress to expand social welfare spending while the charities themselves were "feeding at the public trough."[36] Entire organizations have been formed to "de-halo" the nonprofit sector in this way, charging that a "new kind of nonprofit organization" has emerged in recent years "dedicated not to voluntary action, but to an expanded government role in our lives."[37] To remedy this, advocates of this view rallied behind the so-called Istook Amendment, which sought to limit the advocacy activity of nonprofit organizations by prohibiting any nonprofit organization receiving government support from using any more than 5 percent of its *total* revenues, not just its public revenues, for advocacy or lobbying activities.

Similar challenges to the legitimacy of nonprofit organizations have arisen from critics who take nonprofits to task for becoming *overly* professional and thus losing touch with those they serve and the communities of which they are a part. This line of argument has a long lineage in American social science, as evidenced by the brilliant analysis by historian Roy Lubove of the professionalization of social work, which led social workers away from social diagnosis, community organizing, and social reform toward a client-focused, medical model of social work practice.[38] More recently, critics on the left have implicated nonprofit organizations more generally in the overprofessionalization of social concerns, which, by redefining basic human needs as "problems" that only professionals can resolve, has alienated people from the helping relationships they could establish with their neighbors and kin. "Through the propagation of belief in authoritative expertise," Northwestern University professor John McKnight has thus recently argued, "professionals cut through the social fabric of community and sow clienthood where citizenship once grew."[39] Critics on the right have been equally derisive of the professionalized human service apparatus, charging it with inflating the cost of dealing with social problems by "crowding out" lower cost alternative service delivery mechanisms that are at least as effective.[40]

These sentiments echo loudly in the Bush administration's 2001 proposal to privilege "faith-based charities" in the distribution of federal assistance. A principal appeal of this idea is the prospect of replacing formal, professionalized nonprofit organizations with informal church groups staffed by well-meaning volunteers. This reinforces a quaint nineteenth-century image of how charitable organizations are supposed to operate, an image that competitive pressures, accountability demands, and technological change have made increasingly untenable.

Coupled with a spate of high-profile scandals in the early 1990s, these criticisms seem to have shaken public confidence in charitable institutions. Surveys taken in 1994 and 1996 found only 33 and 37 percent of respondents, respectively, expressing "a great deal" or "quite a lot" of confidence in nonprofit human service agencies, well behind the proportions expressing similar levels of confidence in the military and small business (see table 3-4).[41] This improved considerably in the latter 1990s, perhaps as a consequence of the perceived success of welfare reform. Yet even at this later date, while a substantial majority of respondents agreed that "charitable organizations play a major role in making our communities better places to live," only 20 percent "strongly agreed" with this statement. And only 10 percent of respondents were willing to agree "strongly" that most charities are "honest and ethical in their use of donated funds." In the wake of September 11, moreover, there is some evidence of a further weakening of public confidence in the charitable sector. Thus, the proportion of respondents reporting "a lot" of confidence in charitable organizations dropped from an already low 25 percent in July 2001 to only 18 percent as of May 2002.[42] All of this suggests that America's nonprofit institutions are delicately balanced on a knife-edge of public support,

Table 3-4. *Public Attitudes toward Charitable Organizations in the United States, 1992–99*

| | 1992–96 | | | 1999 | |
| | Percent expressing a great deal or quite a lot of confidence | | | Percent expressing confidence | |
Institutions	1992	1994	1996	A great deal	A great deal or quite a lot
Youth development	48	47	50	33	72
Human services	37	33	37	29	68
Religious organizations	47	50	55	32	61
Private higher education	49	48	57	23	59
Military	49	49	54	22	57
Small business	46	53	56	16	55
Health organizations	40	36	39	15	43
Local government	24	23	31	9	33
State government	19	21	26	8	31
Federal government	18	19	23	8	27
Major corporations	19	22	24	7	29

Source: Independent Sector, *Giving and Volunteering in the United States, 1999* (Washington: Independent Sector, 1999), pp. 3, 5.

with most people willing to grant them the benefit of the doubt, but with a strong undercurrent of uncertainty and concern.[43] As a consequence, a handful of highly visible scandals—such as the United Way scandal of the early 1990s, the New Era Philanthropy scandal of the mid-1990s, or the Red Cross difficulties in the wake of September 11—can have an impact that goes well beyond their actual significance.

The Human Resource Challenge

Inevitably, fiscal stress and public ambivalence toward the nonprofit sector have taken their toll on the sector's human resources. To be sure, recent research has confirmed what many nonprofit experts have long believed—that the nonprofit sector, as one expert recently put it, "has the healthiest workforce in America."[44] More than government or business, nonprofit organizations give their employees a feeling of purpose and offer work experiences that are challenging, meaningful, and engaging. But the sector's ability to attract, and more seriously to retain, talented staff seems increasingly at risk. Of particular concern are problems of burn-out produced by expanded expectations in a context of insufficient resources. Also problematic are the limited opportunities that nonprofit organizations offer for advancement due to the flat nature of many of the organizations. Finally, the private sector and government are fast moving to adopt many of the features that have long given nonprofit organizations such an appeal as places of work—their commitment to mission, to public service, and to a sense of meaning and purpose. They are thus making themselves more competitive with nonprofit workplaces in these terms as well.

Experts in the child welfare field have thus recently identified "staff turnover" as "perhaps the most important problem" facing the field, and cite "stress, . . . overwhelming accountability requirements, and concern over liability" as the principal causes.[45] Similar problems afflict the international relief field, due to the explosion of complex humanitarian crises that blend enormous relief challenges with complicated political and military conflicts.[46]

Especially difficult have been the recruitment and retention of frontline service workers for whom salary, benefit, and safety issues are particularly important. Although there is some evidence that nonprofit wage levels exceed those in for-profit firms in the same field, they are often below those of government agencies. [47] New opportunities in the for-profit sector have also drawn social work personnel into private practice and away from nonprofit human service agencies.

Retention of managerial personnel has also grown increasingly problematic. One study of graduates of public policy programs reports, for example, that the proportion of these public-spirited young people who took their first jobs in nonprofit organizations doubled between the early 1970s and the early 1990s. However, the nonprofit sector's retention rate for these personnel has declined over time, with more turning to the for-profit sector as an alternative.[48] Of special concern is the turnover of talent and burn-out at the executive director level. The identity conflict that afflicts the nonprofit sector as a consequence of the squeeze between increased competition and declining public trust comes most centrally to rest on the person of the nonprofit executive director. Executive directors who came into the field to pursue the social missions of their agencies find themselves expected to function instead as aggressive entrepreneurs leading outward-oriented enterprises able to attract paying customers while retaining the allegiance of socially committed donors and boards, all of this in a context of growing public scrutiny and mistrust. According to one recent study, a surprising two-thirds of the executive directors in a national sample of nonprofit agencies were in their first executive director position, and over half of these had held the job for four years or less. Although most reported enjoying their jobs, a third indicated an intention to leave within two years, and even among those likely to take another job in the nonprofit sector, only half indicated that their next job was likely to be as an executive director.[49]

Leadership recruitment has become a particular challenge in the arts field, as the pressures of fund-raising and marketing drive arts-oriented personnel from the field. Reflecting this, as Margaret Wyszomirski reports, the vacancy rate for art museum directors hit a fifteen-year high in 1999, with twenty directorships at prominent museums open.[50] More generally, a study of northern California nonprofit organizations found that vacancy rates averaging 8 percent of the work force have become the norm, yet few agencies have human resource staff in position to handle this turnover challenge.[51]

Summary

In short, nonprofit America has confronted a difficult set of challenges over the recent past, and many of these challenges seem likely to persist, or to intensify, in the immediate future. Fiscal stress, increased competition, rapidly changing technology, and new accountability expectations have significantly expanded the pressures under which these organizations must work, and this has affected the public support these organizations enjoy and their ability to attract and hold staff.

But challenges are not all that nonprofit America has confronted in the recent past. It has also had the benefit of a number of crucial opportunities, many of which also seem likely to persist. It is to these opportunities that we therefore must turn.

4

The Opportunities

Side by side with the significant challenges it has faced over the recent past, nonprofit America has also confronted an important range of opportunities. To be sure, the presence of opportunities is no guarantee that they will be seized. What is more, opportunities can bring their own risks. Yet no account of the state of nonprofit America can be complete without examining the unusual opportunities that have existed. Four of these in particular deserve special attention.[1]

Social and Demographic Shifts

In the first place, nonprofit America has been the beneficiary of a significant range of social and demographic shifts that have increased not only the need but also the demand for its services, and that may hold the prospect for reducing some of its serious human resource problems. Included among these shifts are the following:

—The doubling of the country's elderly population between 1960 and 2000 and the prospect that there will be four times as many elderly Americans in 2025 as there were in 1960.

—The jump in the labor force participation rate for women, particularly married women, from less than 20 percent in 1960 to 64 percent in 1998.[2]

—The doubling of the country's divorce rate from one in every four marriages in the 1960s to one in every two marriages in the 1980s and thereafter; and a resulting sharp jump in the number of children involved in divorces from less than 500,000 in 1960 to over 1 million per year in the 1980s and 1990s.[3]

—A fivefold increase in the number of out-of-wedlock births, from roughly 225,000 in 1960 to more than 1.25 million per year by the mid-1990s.[4]

—The doubling that occurred in the number of refugees admitted to the United States, from 718,000 between 1966 and 1980 to 1.6 million during the next fifteen years.[5]

Taken together, these and other sociodemographic changes have expanded the demand for many of the services that nonprofit organizations have traditionally provided, such as child day care, home health and nursing home care for the elderly, family counseling, foster care, relocation assistance, and substance abuse treatment and prevention. The pressure on the foster care system alone, for example, has ballooned as the number of children in foster care doubled between the early 1980s and the early 1990s. At the same time, the welfare reform legislation enacted in 1996, with its stress on job readiness, created additional demand for the services that nonprofits typically offer. What is more, the demand for these services has spread well beyond the poor and now encompasses middle-class households with resources to pay for them, a phenomenon that one analyst has called "the transformation of social services."[6] Indeed, the acceleration of modern life and the pressures on two-career families has led to what Atul Dighe refers to as the "outsourcing" of key aspects of family life, from child day care to tutoring and party arranging.[7] Since nonprofit organizations are actively engaged in many of these fields, they stand to gain from this trend.

Equally important is the emergence of what Dighe, following demographers Paul Ray and Sherry Ruth Anderson, calls the "Cultural Creatives," a growing subgroup of the population that now numbers as many as 50 million people.[8] Cultural Creatives differ from both "Moderns" and "Traditionalists," the two other dominant population groups in America, by virtue of their preference for holistic thinking, their cosmopolitanism, their social activism, and their insistence on finding a better balance between work and personal values than the Moderns seem to have found. Though they have yet to develop a full self-consciousness, Cultural Creatives are powerfully attracted to the mission orientation of the nonprofit sector, and could well help fill the sector's growing gap in executive talent.

The New Philanthropy

Also working to the benefit of the nonprofit sector are a series of developments potentially affecting private philanthropy. The first of these is the *intergenerational transfer of wealth* between the Depression-era generation and the postwar baby boomers that is anticipated over the next forty years. Estimated to range anywhere from $10 trillion to $40 trillion, this wealth accumulated in the hands of the Depression-era generation as a consequence of their relatively high propensity to save, their fortuitous investment during the 1950s and 1960s in relatively low-cost houses that then escalated in value during the real estate boom of the 1970s, and the stock market surge of the 1980s and 1990s, which substantially boosted the value of their investments.[9] Contributing as well has been the *new wealth* created by the dot.com economy and other powerful economic trends and policies that substantially increased income levels at the upper end of the income scale during the 1980s and 1990s, accentuating income inequalities but leaving substantial sums of money in the hands of significant numbers of people. Between 1979 and 1992, for example, the share of the nation's wealth controlled by the top 1 percent of households climbed from 20 percent to over 40 percent. Indeed, one-third of the projected intergenerational transfer is expected to go to 1 percent of the baby boom generation, for an average inheritance of $1.6 million per person among this select few.[10]

To be sure, the lengthening life expectancy noted above may dissipate much of this wealth in heavy health care and nursing home expenses. What is more, the stock market meltdown of 1999–2003 provides a powerful reminder of the ephemeral quality of much of the presumed new wealth. Nevertheless, with so much money "in play," substantial opportunities likely exist for the expansion of charitable bequests. The fact that 60 percent of the midsize and larger foundations in existence as of 1999 were created in the 1980s and 1990s certainly lends credence to this belief,[11] though legislation passed in 2001 that would phase out the estate tax and thus eliminate the major financial incentive for forming foundations may put a damper on the extent to which philanthropy will benefit from these developments.

Also encouraging for nonprofit prospects are the new strategies of corporate social involvement that have surfaced in recent years, and the greater corporate willingness to engage in partnerships and collaborations with nonprofit organizations that has resulted from them. Although corporate giving growth has proved far more disappointing than many hoped in the early 1980s, numerous corporations have begun integrating social responsibility activities into their overall corporate business strategies. This has been done in part out of altruistic motives, but in part also out of a recognition that such relationships can serve corporate strategic goals—by winning consumer confidence, ensuring corporations a "license to operate" in the face of increasingly mobilized consumers, workers, and environmentalists, and promoting employee loyalty and morale.[12] As such, these initiatives have a more secure base than altruism alone can provide. The result has been to make corporate managers available to nonprofit organizations not simply as donors, but as allies and collaborators in a wide range of socially important missions, from improving the well-being of children to protecting natural resources. While nonprofit reputations may be put at risk through such relationships, there are also intriguing possibilities for extremely productive partnerships.

Greater Visibility and Policy Salience

Another factor working to the advantage of nonprofit organizations has been a recent spate of political developments that has substantially increased their visibility. For one thing, the policy environment ushered in by the elections of Margaret Thatcher in the United Kingdom and Ronald Reagan in the United States brought nonprofit organizations out of the obscurity to which the rise of the welfare state had consigned them over the previous half-century. Conservative politicians like Thatcher and Reagan needed an explanation for how social problems would be handled once government social welfare protections were cut, and the nonprofit sector offered a highly convenient one. Suddenly, attention to the nonprofit sector and philanthropy became a central part of the policy dialogue, even though conservatives had to overlook in the process the inconvenient fact that the nonprofit organizations they were championing were largely funded by the very government social welfare programs they were cutting. When the policy pendulum swung back to the left, as it did with the election of Tony Blair in the United Kingdom and Bill Clinton in the United States, nonprofit organizations remained very much on the policy screen, as evidenced by the "third way" rhetoric in the United Kingdom, the "reinventing government" paradigm in the United States, and similar formulations in Europe, which view active partnerships between government and the civil society sector as an alternative to relying solely on either the market or the state.[13]

Nonprofit organizations also gained visibility as a result of the collapse of communism in Central Europe in the latter 1980s and the proliferation of complex humanitarian crises in much of the developing world.[14] In both cases nonprofit organizations have been prominently involved, stimulating change and offering alternative mechanisms of response. More recently, these organizations have benefited from the growing concerns about the state of civic engagement in the United States. This is so because nonprofit organizations have been identified as crucial contributors to "social capital," to the bonds of trust and reciprocity thought to be necessary to sustain civic involvement. Encouragement of a vital nonprofit sector has thus come to be seen as a critical prerequisite for a healthy democracy.[15]

Finally, the events of September 11 also seem to have increased the public's recognition of the nonprofit sector. As noted earlier, nonprofit organizations were visible participants in the response to this tragedy. Beyond this, the September 11 tragedy seems to have reawakened Americans to the importance of the functions that nonprofit institutions perform, functions such as serving those in need, building community, and encouraging values of care and concern.

Resumption of Government Social Welfare Spending Growth

Finally, and perhaps most important, government social welfare spending, which had stalled, and in some cases reversed course, in the early 1980s, resumed its growth in the late 1980s and into the 1990s. As noted in table 4-1, total public social welfare spending increased 36 percent in real, inflation-adjusted dollars between 1985 and 1995, compared to a 24 percent increase in the country's real GDP.[16] Particularly notable was the 69 percent growth in health spending, but significant increases were recorded in housing, education, and social service spending as well—and these trends have continued through the 1990s. Five factors seem to have been responsible for this growth.

Broadening of Federal Entitlement Spending

In the first place, as noted earlier, spending under the basic federal, and federal-state, entitlement programs for health and income assistance

Table 4-1. *Growth in Real Government Social Welfare Spending, 1985–95*
Percent

Function	Total	Federal	State and local
Pensions	18	13	40
Income assistance	27	34	7
Health	69	67	73
Education	40	9	43
Elementary, secondary	–34	–34	–34
Higher	36	–23	31
Housing	54	63	–10
Social services	23	5	49
Total	36	30	45
Excluding pensions, health	37	29	40

Source: U.S. Social Security Administration, *Annual Statistical Supplement to the Social Security Bulletin* (U.S. Department of Health and Human Services, 2000), pp. 119–222.

grew rapidly during this period. This was due in important part to the steady broadening of eligibility under these programs. For example, coverage under the federal Supplemental Security Income program, which was originally created to provide income support to the elderly poor, ballooned from 4.1 million recipients in 1980 to 6.6 million by 1999, largely as a result of aggressive efforts to enroll disabled people, including children and youth, in the program following a 1990 Supreme Court decision that liberalized SSI eligibility requirements. The number of children covered by SSI increased from 71,000 in 1974 to over 1 million in 1996 as a consequence, boosting expenditures in real terms from $16.4 billion in 1980 to $30.2 billion in 1999.[17] And since SSI coverage entitles participants to coverage under Medicaid, the federal health care financing program for the poor, this increase translated into Medicaid growth as well.

But this was not the only source of Medicaid eligibility expansion. Medicaid coverage was extended to 50 distinct subgroups during the latter 1980s and early 1990s, including many more children and pregnant women as well as the homeless, newly legalized aliens, AIDS sufferers, recipients of adoption assistance and foster care, and broader

Table 4-2. *Growth in Federal Entitlement Program Spending, 1980–99*

Program	Spending (billions of constant 1999 dollars)[a]		Percentage change 1980–99
	1980	1999	
Medicare	79.9	212.0	165
Medicaid[b]	56.8	189.5	222
Supplemental Security Income[b]	9.5	30.9	225
Total	146.2	432.4	196
U.S. gross domestic product	4,900.9	8,856.5	81

Source: U.S. House of Representatives, Committee on Ways and Means, *2000 Green Book: Background Material and Data on Programs within the Jurisdiction of the Committee on Ways and Means,* 106th Cong. 2d sess. (October 6, 2000), pp. 100, 912, 214; Council of Economic Advisers, *Economic Report of the President, 2002* (Washington: Executive Office of the President, 2002), table B-2.

a. Based on chain-type price deflators for the service component of personal consumption expenditures.

b. Includes both federal and state spending.

categories of the disabled and the elderly. Between 1980 and 1998 as a consequence, Medicaid coverage increased from 21.6 million people to 40.6 million.[18]

Expanded eligibility was not the only source of entitlement program growth, however. Also important were extensions in the range of services these programs cover. Thus, skilled nursing care, home health care, hospice care, and kidney dialysis services became eligible for Medicare coverage; while mandatory Medicaid coverage was extended to intermediate care for the mentally retarded, home health care, family planning, clinic care, child welfare services, and rehabilitation services. Coupled with an expansion of services made eligible for Medicaid coverage at state option (for example, physical therapy, medical social worker counseling, case management, transportation), these changes transformed Medicaid from a relatively narrow health and nursing home program into a veritable social service entitlement program.[19]

Reflecting these changes, as shown in table 4-2, spending on the major federal entitlement programs jumped nearly 200 percent in real terms between 1980 and 1999, more than twice the 81 percent real growth in the U.S. gross domestic product. Although reimbursement rates under these programs were still often not sufficient to cover the full costs of the services, the expansion in the pool of resources available was substantial.

New Federal Initiatives

In addition to expanding existing programs, federal policymakers also created a variety of new programs to address long-standing or newly emerging social ills. For example, four federal child care programs were enacted in 1988 and 1990 alone, and special programs were added as well for homeless people, AIDS sufferers, children and youth, people with disabilities, voluntarism promotion, drug and alcohol treatment, and home health care. Federal spending on the homeless, for example, went from virtually zero in 1986 to $1.2 billion in fiscal 2000.[20]

Greater State Activism

Renewed federal activism was mirrored, and in some cases anticipated, moreover, by activism at the state and local levels. In some cases, state and local governments replaced cuts in federal spending with their own new or expanded programs. This was the case, for example, in the arts field, where state and local governments more than made up for cuts in National Endowment for the Arts grants to state and local arts agencies.[21] In other cases, states found new veins of federal funding to tap as old ones ran dry.

The most striking example here is what became known as the "Medicaid maximization strategy," under which programs formerly funded entirely by the states, or by federal discretionary programs subjected to Reagan-era budget cuts, were reconfigured to make them eligible for funding under the more lucrative and still-growing Medicaid or SSI programs. Mental health, mental retardation, maternal and child health, rehabilitation, and AIDS services were special targets for this strategy, particularly as Medicaid expanded eligibility for pregnant women and children, and SSI (and hence Medicaid) expanded coverage for AIDS patients and the disabled.[22] Finally, a growing number of states opted to exploit the flexibilities built into the Medicaid program to extend care beyond the required minimums in order to address key social problems, such as teen pregnancy and drug abuse. Thus, for example, as of 1998, thirty-five states as well as the District of Columbia had agreed to extend coverage to the so-called "medically needy" (that is, individuals who are otherwise eligible for Medicaid coverage but who exceed the Medicaid income limits).[23] Twenty-two agreed to offer hospice care, twenty-six agreed to cover skilled nursing facilities for individuals under twenty-one, and thirty-one agreed to provide rehabilitative services.[24] Taken together, these changes explain why state and local social welfare spending grew even faster than federal spending between 1985 and 1995 (45 percent versus 30 percent), as reflected in table 4-1. [25]

The Welfare Reform Windfall

A fourth factor contributing to the recent expansion of government spending in fields where nonprofits are active was the passage of federal welfare reform legislation in 1996 and the subsequent change in the welfare caseload. The Personal Responsibility and Work Opportunity Reconciliation Act (PRWORA) of 1996 essentially replaced the existing program of entitlement grants to states to help cover welfare payments to dependent children and families with a fixed federal grant that was guaranteed for six years, during which states were required to move welfare recipients into paying jobs.

As part of this legislation, states were permitted to use a portion of these funds to finance not simply welfare payments but also a variety of work readiness, child care, and human service activities. The result was to transform the existing welfare program into "a broad human services funding stream."[26] When welfare rolls began to fall sharply in the late 1990s, thanks to the economic boom then in progress and the stringent work requirements built into the new law, states found themselves with a fiscal windfall since their welfare grants from the federal government were locked in at the preexisting levels while their payments to recipients declined.[27] States were thus able to invest the savings in a variety of service programs designed to prepare even more welfare recipients for work. By 1999, for example, spending on cash and work-based assistance under the welfare program had fallen to 60 percent of the total funds available, leaving 40 percent for a variety of child care, work readiness, drug abuse treatment, and related purposes. As a result, the social welfare system was unexpectedly awash with funds.

New Tools

Finally, given the prevailing climate of tax cuts and hostility to expanded government spending throughout the 1980s and early 1990s, policymakers increasingly responded to social welfare and related needs by relying more heavily on unconventional tools of government action, such as loan guarantees and tax subsidies, which do not appear as visibly in the budget.[28] The use of such tools is by no means entirely new, of course. The deduction for medical expenses and the exclusion of scholarship income, for example, have long been established features of the tax code. But the use of such tools in fields where nonprofits are active expanded considerably in the 1990s with the addition or extension of programs such as the child care tax credit, the credit for student loan interest payments, the Low-Income Housing Tax Credit, and the new market tax credit. As of fiscal 2001, as table 4-3 shows, these alternative tools accounted for another $315.2 billion in federal assistance in fields where nonprofits are active. As reflected in table 4-4, this represents a 123 percent increase in constant dollars over what was available through these tools a decade earlier, a rate of increase that exceeded even that achieved by the spending programs in these same fields. In many fields, such as day care, the indirect subsidies available through the tax system now exceed those available through the outright spending programs.[29] What is more, the new tools generally deliver their benefits to consumers rather than

Table 4-3. *Major Federal Tax Expenditure and Loan Programs of Relevance to Nonprofits, 2001*

Program	Millions of U.S. dollars
Tax expenditures (outlay equivalent)	
Insurance companies owned by nps	300
Low-income housing credit	4,360
Empowerment zone	380
New markets tax credit	20
Scholarship income exclusion	1,330
HOPE tax credit	5,300
Lifetime learning tax credit	3,030
Student loan interest deduction	460
State prepaid tuition plans	250
Student loan bond interest deduction	330
Nonprofit education facilities bond interest	770
Parental exemption for students	1,120
Charitable contribution deduction	53,260
Employer educational assistance	320
Employer-provided child care	950
Adopted foster care assistance	220
Adoption credit	160
Child credit	26,460
Child care credit	3,560
Employer medical insurance contributions	106,750
Self-employed medical insurance	1,900
Workers compensation insurance premiums	5,900
Medical expense deduction	4,990
Hospital construction bond interest	1,580
Public purpose state/local bond interest	33,100
Parsonage allowance deduction	400
Subtotal	257,200
Loan guarantee commitments	
Health center guaranteed loan	7
Family education loan program	34,705
Community development loan guarantees	244
Student Loan Marketing Association	3,819
Subtotal	38,775
Direct loan obligations	
Historically black college capital financing	16
Direct student loan program	19,219
Community development financial institutions fund	12
Community development credit union revolving fund	10
Subtotal	19,257
Total	315,232

Source: Analytical Perspectives, *Budget of the United States Government, Fiscal Year 2003* (Washington, D.C.: U.S. Government Printing Office, 2002), pp. 99–101, 213–33.

Table 4-4. *Growth in Federal Tax Expenditure and Loan Programs of Relevance to Nonprofits, 1990–2001*

Type of program	Amount (billions of constant 2001 dollars)		Percentage change, 1990–2001
	1990	2001	
Tax expenditures	114.4	257.2	125
Direct loan commitments	0.1	19.3	17,000
Loan guarantee commitments	26.9	38.8	44
Total	141.4	315.3	123

Source: *Special Analyses, Budget of the U.S. Government, FY 1990* (Government Printing Office, 1989), pp. F70-87, G44-49; *Analytical Perspective, Budget of the U.S. Government Fiscal Year 2003* (Government Printing Office, 2002), pp. 99–101; 212–33.

producers, making it necessary for nonprofits to market their services in order to benefit.

To be sure, the expansion of government spending that occurred from the late 1980s though the 1990s did not affect all fields in which nonprofits are active. Public spending on higher education, for example, lost ground, though the creation of a direct student loan program and the continued expansion of tax and credit programs for higher education softened some of the blow. In addition, the shift in the character of public sector support from producer-side subsidies to consumer-side subsidies meant that access to it was more difficult, necessitating more intensive marketing efforts. Nevertheless, the increase that took place in government spending in fields where nonprofits are active was striking, creating another important opportunity for the sector.

Summary

In short, American nonprofit organizations have not only been buffeted by a variety of significant challenges. They have also enjoyed a number of important opportunities. What is really important is not just the scope of these competing pressures, however, but how the organizations have responded. It is to this topic that we now turn.

5

The Nonprofit Response:
A Story of Resilience

How has nonprofit America responded to the extraordinary combination of challenges and opportunities it has faced over the past decade and a half? Has the sector been able to cope with the challenges and take advantage of the opportunities? To what extent and with what consequences for its current health and character, and for its likely evolution? It is to these questions that we now turn.

Judging from the conventional wisdom about the responsiveness of nonprofit organizations, we should not expect a very positive report. "Profit-making organizations are more flexible [than nonprofits] with respect to the deployment and redeployment of resources," management experts Rosabeth Moss Kanter and David V. Summers thus wrote in 1987.[1] Nonprofits are not to be trusted, Professor Regina Herzlinger similarly explained to readers of the *Harvard Business Review* in 1996, because they lack the three basic accountability measures that ensure effective and efficient operations in the business world: the self-interest of owners, competition, and the ultimate bottom-line measure of profitability.[2]

Contrary to these conventional beliefs, however, the past ten to fifteen years have constituted a period of extraordinary resilience and adaptability on the part of America's nonprofit sector. Although largely unheralded, nonprofit America has undergone a quiet revolution, a massive process of reinvention and re-engineering that is still very much under way. To be sure, the resulting changes are hardly universal: change has been more pronounced in some fields than in others, and even within fields substantial variation exists among agencies of different sizes and orientations. What is more, there are serious questions about whether the resulting changes are in a wholly desirable direction, or whether they have exposed the sector to unacceptable risks. Although important shadings are needed to do justice to the considerable diversity that exists, however, there is no denying the dominant picture of resilience, adaptation, and change. More specifically, ten threads of change are apparent.

Overall Sector Growth

Perhaps the most vivid evidence of the nonprofit sector's resilience is the striking record of recent sector growth. Between 1977 and 1997, as shown in table 5-1, the revenues of America's nonprofit organizations increased 144 percent after adjusting for inflation, nearly twice the 81 percent growth rate of the nation's economy. Nonprofit revenue growth was particularly robust among arts and culture organizations, social service organizations, and health organizations, in each of which the rate of growth was at least twice that of the U.S. economy. However, even the most laggard components of the nonprofit sector (education, civic, and social organizations) grew at a rate that equaled or exceeded overall U.S. economic growth.[3]

Evidence of the vibrancy of the nonprofit sector extends well beyond financial indicators, which are heavily influenced by the performance of the largest organizations. Equally revealing is the record of recent organizational formation. Between 1977 and 1997 the

Table 5-1. *Real Growth in Nonprofit Revenue, by Subsector, 1977–97*
Percent

Field	Percentage of total, 1977	Percentage change, 1977–97	Share of change, 1977–97
Health	47	167	55
Education	25	82	14
Social services	9	213	14
Civic, social	4	79	2
Arts, culture	2	280	3
Religion	13	135	12
Total	100	144	100
U.S. gross domestic product		81	

Source: Data on nonprofit organizations adapted from Murray S. Weitzman and others, *The New Nonprofit Almanac and Desk Reference* (San Francisco: Jossey-Bass, 2002), pp. 96–97; data on U.S. gross domestic product from Council of Economic Advisers, *Economic Report of the President, 2002* (Washington: Executive Office of the President, 2002).

number of 501(c)(3) and 501(c)(4) organizations registered with the Internal Revenue Service increased by 115 percent, or about 23,000 organizations a year.[4] By comparison, the number of business organizations increased only 76 percent during this same period. Moreover, the rate of nonprofit organization formation seems to have accelerated in more recent years, jumping from an average of 15,000 a year between 1977 and 1987 to more than 27,000 a year between 1987 and 1997, and this despite increased pressures for organizational mergers. Evidently, Americans are still finding in the nonprofit sector a convenient outlet for a wide assortment of social, economic, political, and cultural concerns.[5]

Marketing to Paying Customers

What accounts for this record of robust growth? One of the central explanations appears to be the success with which American nonprofits took advantage of the favorable demographic and social trends they confronted to market their services to a clientele increasingly able to

Table 5-2. *Changing Structure of Nonprofit Revenue, 1977–97*
Percent

Revenue source	Total percentage change, 1977–97	Share of total				Share of revenue growth, 1977–97	
		All nonprofits		Nonprofits excluding religion		All nonprofits	Nonprofits excluding religion
		1977	1997	1977	1997		
Fees, charges	145	46	47	51	51	47	51
Government	195	27	33	31	37	37	42
Philanthropy	90	27	20	18	12	16	8
Total	144	100	100	100	100	100	100

Source: See table 5-1.

afford them. Reflecting this, even with religious congregations included, fees and charges accounted for nearly half (47 percent) of the growth in nonprofit revenue between 1977 and 1997—more than any other source (see table 5-2).

To be sure, not all components of the nonprofit sector relied equally heavily on fees and charges to finance their operations during this period, as shown in table 5-3. What is striking about this period of nonprofit development, however, is how extensively reliance on fee income has spread throughout the sector. After adjusting for inflation, the fee income of arts and culture organizations jumped 272 percent, of civic organizations 220 percent, and of social service organizations over 500 percent between 1977 and 1997, thus accounting for 46, 53, and 35 percent, respectively, of the growth of these agencies. Even religious congregations boosted their commercial income during this period, largely from the sale or rental of church property.[6]

Not only did nonprofits boost their fee revenues from existing clients, they also apparently pursued middle-class clientele into the Sun Belt and the suburbs. This is evident in the growing suburbanization of philanthropy during the 1980s reported by economist Julian Wolpert, and in the geographic spread of nonprofit employment reported by the Johns Hopkins Nonprofit Employment Data Project.[7]

Table 5-3. *Growth of Nonprofit Fee Income, by Subsector, 1977–97*
Percent

Field	Percentage change, 1977–97	Share of total revenue		Share of revenue growth, 1977–97
		1977	1997	
Health	162	53	52	52
Education	77	67	65	63
Social services	587	13	28	35
Civic	220	19	34	53
Arts, culture	272	47	46	46
Religion	163	14	16	17
Total	145	46	47	47
Excluding religion	144	51	51	51

Source: See table 5-1.

Seventy percent of the substantial growth of nonprofit employment in the state of Maryland between 1989 and 1999, for example, took place in the Baltimore and Washington suburbs, whereas the city of Baltimore, which started the period with nearly half of the state's nonprofit employment, accounted for only 17 percent of the growth.

Clearly, market forces have intruded into the nonprofit sector well beyond the fields of health and higher education to which they were formerly mostly confined. And the organizations in this broader array of fields have demonstrated an equal capacity to respond to them.

Successful Pursuit of Public Funds

Not only have nonprofit organizations in an ever wider range of fields managed to adapt themselves to the new market opportunities they are facing, but they have also proved adept in coping with the new public funding terrain that has evolved in recent years. As a result, despite the rhetoric of retrenchment that has characterized this period, one of the most striking features of the past decade and a half has been an enormous growth in nonprofit revenue from public sector sources.

Table 5-4. *Growth in Nonprofit Revenue from Government, by Subsector,*
1977–97
Percent

Field	Percentage change, 1977–97	Share of total revenue		Share of revenue growth, 1977–97
		1977	1997	
Health	248	32	42	48
Education	94	18	19	21
Social services	200	54	52	51
Civic	8	50	30	5
Arts, culture	214	12	10	9
Religion	0	0	0	0
Total	195	27	33	37
Excluding religion	195	31	37	42

Source: See table 5-1.

As noted in table 5-2, government support to the nonprofit sector increased by 195 percent in real terms between 1977 and 1997, proportionally more than any other source, and these figures do not include the windfall from welfare reform discussed earlier. Government accounted for 37 percent of the sector's substantial growth during this period, boosting its share of the total from 27 percent in 1977 to 33 percent in 1997. And with religious congregations excluded (since they do not receive much government support), the government contribution to sector growth came to 42 percent, boosting government's share of the sector's revenue from 31 percent in 1977 to 37 percent in 1997.

Not all segments of the sector benefited equally from this expanding government support, of course. The major beneficiaries were nonprofit health, social service, and arts organizations, all of which lifted their government support by 200 percent or more after adjusting for inflation (see table 5-4). Government revenue growth was less robust for education organizations, although it still exceeded the overall growth of the domestic economy; while for civic organizations it barely kept pace with inflation, perhaps confirming fears that the real thrust of the budget cutting of the 1980s and early 1990s was to "defund the left."

The proximate cause of this extraordinary growth in nonprofit revenue from government was, of course, the expansion in government spending that occurred in fields where nonprofits are active. At least as important, however, has been the skill with which nonprofit organizations adapted to the shifts they faced in the *forms* of public support. Social service agencies had to be particularly nimble in adjusting to the new realities as states shifted their social service spending from stagnant or declining discretionary grant programs to the rapidly growing Medicaid and SSI programs, both of which deliver their benefits to clients and therefore require agencies to master new marketing, billing, and reimbursement management skills. That they successfully did so is evident in the sizable 200 percent increase in public funding that they achieved.

Similarly impressive was the success of nonprofit housing and community development organizations in taking advantage of the new Low-Income Housing Tax Credit designed to stimulate the flow of private investment capital into low-income housing. This success was due in large part to the role that a skilled set of nonprofit intermediary organizations played in packaging the resulting tax credits and marketing them to for-profit financial institutions, generating in the process a substantial flow of private capital into the hands of community-based organizations in this field. [8] In view of the capital deficiencies facing nonprofit organizations in many fields, this record holds important lessons for the sector in general.

This significant expansion of government support has also had its downsides, of course. Particularly problematic has been the tendency for Medicaid (and to some extent Medicare) reimbursement rates to fall behind the actual costs of delivering the services they are intended to support.[9] For-profit vendors can respond to these cuts by pulling out of the affected lines of business, but nonprofits often find this difficult. As a consequence, nonprofit organizations often end up having to use scarce private charitable resources to subsidize their federally funded services.

Even so, the success with which nonprofit organizations have adapted to the new government funding realities is another demonstration of the sector's recent resilience and adaptability. More than that, it provides a further indication of the sector's growing "marketization," since so much of the government aid now takes the form of "consumer-side" subsidies. When this voucher-type government support is added to the fee income that nonprofits receive, as it is in the data on "program service revenue" that nonprofit organizations report to the Internal Revenue Service, it turns out that two-thirds (67 percent) of the reported income of nonprofit 501(c)(3) organizations as of 1998 came from such "commercial" sources. And with investment income included as well, the commercial total is over 75 percent. Even among human service nonprofits, the combination of consumer-side government subsidies plus fee income accounted for over half (54 percent) of total revenue in 1998.[10]

Much of this growth in government support is now at risk, however, as a consequence of the new budget stringency that surfaced in 2001. In response, states have moved quickly to begin reversing the expansions of eligibility and coverage under Medicaid and related programs that fueled the growth of government support to nonprofit human service agencies over the previous decade.[11] Tax cuts enacted by Congress in 2003 at the behest of the Bush administration, moreover, seem likely to intensify this trend.[12]

The Revolution in Charitable Fundraising

Accompanying the growing sophistication that nonprofit organizations have demonstrated in pursuing fee income and tapping government support has been the increased creativity they have displayed in raising charitable contributions. The past twenty years have witnessed a growing professionalization of charitable fund-raising, and with it, a proliferation of mechanisms for generating charitable resources. One reflection of this is the emergence and growth of specialized organizations catering to the new fund-raising profession—the National Society of Fund-Raising Executives (1960), now the Association of Fund-Raising Professionals (AFP); the Council for the Advancement and Support of Education (1974); the Association for Healthcare Philanthropy (1967); and the National Committee for Planned Giving (1988). As recently as 1979, AFP, the largest of these organizations, boasted only 1,899 members. By 1999 it claimed more than 20,000; and the National Committee for Planned Giving, a more specialized body, itself had 11,000.[13]

This growth of a fund-raising profession has had the fortuitous result of helping to democratize charitable giving, moving it from an almost exclusive focus on the wealthy to a broader mass base.[14] The vehicle for this has not been individual solicitors standing on street corners in the old Salvation Army model, however. Rather, the technology of charitable giving has also been transformed through the development of such devices as workplace solicitation, telethons, direct mail campaigns, telephone solicitation, and, most recently, e-philanthropy. Entire organizations have surfaced to manage this process of extracting funds. Included here are entities such as United Way, the various health appeals (for example, the American Cancer Society, the American Heart Association), and the nation's growing network of community foundations.

As noted, for-profit businesses have also increasingly gotten into the act, building on a tradition of for-profit fund-raising firms stretching back to at least the 1930s.[15] The new actors are financial service companies that have capitalized on their mastery of finance to popularize a variety of relatively new "planned giving" mechanisms. These instruments allow donors to earn tax-sheltered income on funds deposited in special "split income" or "charitable remainder" trusts during their lifetimes or the lifetimes of designated beneficiaries, and then to contribute the remaining assets to charities at their death without having to pay estate taxes. The for-profit investment firms have also actively promoted a variety of "donor-advised funds," which give donors the opportunity to retain control over assets deposited for charitable purposes while securing tax advantages at the full appreciated value of the contributed assets at the time of contribution. By 2000, the largest of these operations—the Fidelity Charitable Gift Fund managed by the Boston-based for-profit investment firm Fidelity Investments—reported assets of $2.4 billion. Partly in response to this competition, nonprofit community foundations and federated funding organizations have also intensified their use of these instruments, boosting the reported assets in donor-advised funds to an estimated $10.4 billion as of 2000.[16] Along with new "donor option" arrangements in traditional federated charitable appeals like United Way, and the emergence of "venture philanthropy," this explosion of donor-advised funds suggests the emergence of an alternative model of institutional philanthropy modeled on the decentralized, entrepreneurial firms that have been the source of much of the new-economy wealth being channeled into charitable activity.[17] As such, it differs from the more bureaucratic forms embodied in the large staffed foundations, which grew out of the more hierarchic enterprises of an earlier era.

This revolution in the technology of charitable fundraising doubtless boosted charitable giving above what it might otherwise have been. It did not, however, counter the effects of other developments, including tax and other policies, working to dampen the growth in giving. For one thing, the new forms of charitable fund-raising are often more costly, requiring heavier administrative expenditures to raise a given quantity of charitable resources. For another, some of the new vehicles delay the transfer of wealth into charitable uses. Donor-advised funds and charitable remainder trusts are essentially holding vats for charitable dollars, and some in the charitable community bewail the resulting reduction in direct contributions to operating charities and in direct contact between donors and recipient organizations that these devices also produce.[18] Whatever the reason, despite the innovations in fundraising techniques, the growth of private charitable giving, while substantial, has not kept pace with the growth of nonprofit revenue more generally. Thus, as shown in table 5-2 above, charitable giving increased 90 percent between 1977 and 1997, well below the growth rate for the other major sources of nonprofit revenue.

As with the other sources of income, the growth in giving varied by subsector, as noted in table 5-5. Especially notable was the above-average growth of private giving in the fields of religion, civic activity, and arts and culture, where private giving accounted for over 40 percent of total revenue growth during this 20-year period. The increase in the case of religion is especially surpising, since public participation in religious organizations declined during this period.[19] By contrast, philanthropic support to the nation's social service agencies grew much more slowly. As a result, the philanthropic share of social service organization income fell from 33 percent in 1977 to 20 percent twenty years later. Philanthropy, it appears, became even more amenities-oriented over this twenty-year period, a trend that is potentially troubling.[20] More generally, philanthropy accounted for only 16 percent of the growth of the sector during this period, and much of this

Table 5-5. *Growth in Nonprofit Revenue from Philanthropy, by Subsector, 1977–97*

Percent

Field	Percentage change, 1977–97	Share of total revenue		Share of revenue growth, 1977–97
		1977	1997	
Health	3	14	6	0
Education	91	15	16	17
Social services	91	33	20	14
Civic	106	31	36	42
Arts, culture	307	41	44	45
Religion	131	86	84	83
Total	90	27	20	16
Excluding religion	62	18	12	8

Source: See table 5-1.

was due to the growth of contributions to religious congregations. With that portion of private giving excluded, philanthropy accounted for only 8 percent of the sector's growth, and its share of sector income declined from 18 to 12 percent.

Although philanthropy grew more robustly in the most recent portion of this period (1992–97) than earlier, any hope this might have triggered about a permanent reversal in the steady decline in giving's share of nonprofit income was dealt a severe setback by the stock market sell-off of 2000–02. Even with the outpouring of post–September 11 benevolence, giving actually declined in real dollar terms in 2001, the latest year for which data are available, and the downturn seems to have extended into 2002 as well.[21]

Expanded Venture Activity

A fifth manifestation of the nonprofit sector's recent resilience has been the sector's increased involvement in commercial ventures. Such ventures differ from the collection of fees for standard nonprofit services in that they entail the creation and sale of products and services primarily for a commercial market. Examples include museum gift shops and online stores, the rental of social halls by churches, and licensing agreements between research universities and commercial firms. Existing law has long allowed nonprofit organizations to engage in such commercial activities so long as they do not become the primary purpose of the organization. Since 1951 the income from such ventures has been subject to corporate income taxation unless it is "related" to the charitable purpose of the organization.

Solid data on the scale of nonprofit venture activity is difficult to locate, since much of it is considered "related" activity and buried in the statistics on fees, but the clear impression from what data exist suggests a substantial expansion over the past two decades. One sign of this is the growth in so-called "unrelated business income" reported to the Internal Revenue Service. Although the IRS has been notoriously liberal in its definition of what constitutes "unrelated," as opposed to "related," business income, the number of charities reporting such income increased by 35 percent between 1990 and 1997, and the amount of income they reported more than doubled.[22] As of 1997, gross unrelated business income reported by nonprofit organizations reached $7.8 billion, an increase of 7 percent over the previous year, following increases of 30 percent a year over the previous two years.

Cultural institutions seem to have been especially inventive in adapting venture activities to their operations, perhaps because they have the clearest "products" to sell. The Guggenheim Museum has even gone global, with franchises in Italy, Germany, and Spain, while elaborate touring exhibitions and shows have also become standard facets of museum, orchestra, and dance company operations. Cultural institutions are also actively exploiting the new digitization technologies, often in collaboration with commercial firms. In the process, arts organizations are being transformed from inward-oriented institutions catering to the artistic interests of their patrons and focused primarily on their collections to outward-oriented enterprises competing for customers in an increasingly commercial market.[23]

Other types of nonprofit organizations are also increasingly involved in commercial-type ventures. Thus, hospitals are investing in parking garages, universities are establishing joint ventures with private biotechnology companies, and social service agencies are operating restaurants and catering businesses. The business activities of nonprofit hospitals have grown especially complex, with elaborate purchasing and marketing consortia linking hospitals, medical practitioners, insurance groups, and equipment suppliers.[24]

Perhaps the most interesting facet of this development is the recent tendency of some nonprofit organizations to utilize business ventures not simply to generate income but to carry out their basic charitable missions. This reflects a broader transformation in prevailing conceptions of the causes of poverty and distress from a focus on providing individuals with needed services to a focus on getting them to work.

Thus, rather than merely training disadvantaged individuals and sending them out into the private labor market, a new class of "social purpose enterprises," or "social ventures," has emerged to employ former drug addicts, inmates, or other disadvantaged persons in actual businesses as a way to build skills, develop self-confidence, and teach work habits.[25] Examples here include the Greyston Bakery in Yonkers, New York, which trains and hires unemployable workers in its gourmet bakery business; the New Community Corporation in Newark, New Jersey, which provides job training and employment to inner-city residents through a network of grocery and convenience stores, restaurants, and print and copy shops; Pioneer Human Services, a nonprofit in Seattle, Washington, that operates an aircraft parts manufacturing facility, food buying and warehousing services, and restaurants; and Bikeable Communities in Long Beach, California, which promotes bicycle use by offering valet and related services to cyclists.[26] In each of these cases, the venture is not a sideline or a mere revenue source but an integral component of the agency's charitable program. The result is a thoroughgoing marriage of market means to charitable purpose and the emergence of a new, hybrid form of nonprofit business.

Adoption of the Enterprise Culture

These developments point, in turn, to a broader and deeper penetration of the market culture into the fabric of nonprofit operations. Nonprofit organizations are increasingly "marketing" their "products," viewing their clients as "customers," segmenting their markets, differentiating their output, identifying their "market niche," formulating "business plans," and generally incorporating the language, and the style, of business management into the operation of their agencies. Indeed, management expert Kevin Kearns argues that nonprofit executives are now "among the most entrepreneurial managers to be found anywhere, including the private for-profit sector."[27]

How fully the culture of the market has been integrated into the operations, as opposed to the rhetoric, of the nonprofit sector is difficult to determine. Paul Light reports that "outcomes measurement," a key part of this market-oriented approach, is in "high tide" or "rising tide" among nonprofits in eighteen of the nineteen states whose non-profit association directors he surveyed, and "marketization" is in roughly the same position in twelve.[28] Certainly the appetite for materials has been robust enough to convince commercial publishers like John Wiley and Sons to invest heavily in the field, producing a booming market in "how-to" books offering nonprofit managers training in "strategic planning," "financial planning, "mission-based management," "social entrepreneurship," "streetsmart financial basics," "strategic communications," "high performance philanthropy," and "high performance organization," to cite just a handful of recent titles.[29] The Drucker Foundation's *Self-Assessment Tool*, with its market-oriented stress on the five questions considered most critical to non-profit-organization performance—"What is our mission? Who is our customer? What does the customer value? What are our results? What is our plan?"—was reportedly purchased by more than 10,000 agencies in the first five years following its publication in 1993, suggesting the interest in business-style management advice within the sector.[30]

More concretely, there is growing evidence that the market culture is affecting organizational practices, organizational structures, and interorganizational behavior. Hospitals, for example, are increasingly advertising their capabilities, universities are investing in off-campus programs, museums and symphonies are establishing venues in shopping centers, and even small community development organizations are engaging in complex real estate syndications. Significant changes are also occurring in the basic structure and governance of nonprofit organizations. Boards are being made smaller and more selective, substituting a corporate model for a more community-based one. Similarly, greater efforts are being made to recruit business leaders onto boards, further solidifying the dominant corporate culture. In addition, the internal structure of organizations is growing more complex. To some extent this is driven by prevailing legal restrictions. Thus, many nonprofit advocacy organizations have created 501(c)(4) subsidiaries to bypass restrictions on their lobbying activity as 501(c)(3) charities.[31] Similarly, nonprofit residential care facilities are segmenting their various programs into separate corporate entities to build legal walls around their separate operations in case of liability challenges. Elsewhere, commercial pressures are pushing organizations in similar directions. Thus hospitals are increasingly creating for-profit subsidiaries and joint ventures with proprietary physician groups or managed care organizations in order to position themselves better in increasingly competitive markets.[32] Universities, freed by the Bayh-Dole Act and subsequent legislation to patent discoveries developed with federal research funds, are turning to similar arrangements to help market the products of university-based scientific research.[33] Behind the comforting facade of relatively homey charities, nonprofit organizations are thus being transformed into complex holding companies, with multiple nonprofit and for-profit subsidiaries and offshoots, significantly complicating the task of operational and financial management and control.

New Business Partnerships

As the culture of the market has spread into the fabric of nonprofit operations, old suspicions between the nonprofit and business sectors have significantly softened, opening the way for nonprofit acceptance of the business community not simply as a source of charitable support but as a legitimate partner for a wide range of nonprofit endeavors. This perspective has been championed by charismatic sector leaders such as Billy Shore, who urge nonprofits to stop thinking about how to get donations and start thinking about how to "market" the considerable "assets" they control, including particularly the asset represented by their reputations.[34] This has meshed nicely with the growing readiness of businesses to forge strategic alliances with nonprofits in order to generate "reputational capital." The upshot has been a notable upsurge in strategic partnerships between nonprofit organizations and businesses.

One early manifestation of this approach was the "cause-related marketing" technique pioneered by American Express in the early 1980s. Under this technique, a nonprofit lends its name to a commercial product in return for a share of the proceeds from the sale of that product. Research has demonstrated that such arrangements bring substantial returns to the companies involved, boosting sales, enhancing company reputations, and buoying employee morale. Coca-Cola, for example, experienced a 490 percent spurt in the sales of its products at 450 Wal-Mart stores in 1997 when it launched a campaign promising to donate 15 cents to Mothers Against Drunk Driving for every soft-drink case it sold. More generally, a 1999 Cone/Roper survey found that two-thirds of Americans have greater trust in companies aligned with a social issue, and more than half of all workers wish their employers would do more to support social causes. This evidence has convinced a growing number of corporations to associate themselves and their products with social causes and the groups actively working on them. Apparel retailer Eddie Bauer has thus entered cause-related marketing arrangements with American Forests, Evian with Bill Shore's Share Our Strength, Liz Claiborne with the Family Violence Prevention Fund, Mattel with Girls Incorporated, Timberland with City Year, and many more. By 1998, such arrangements were generating $1.5 billion in marketing fees for the nonprofit organizations involved.[35]

Many of these cause-related marketing relationships have subsequently evolved, moreover, into broader partnerships that mobilize corporate personnel, finances, and know-how in support of nonprofit activities. The most successful of these efforts deliver benefits to both the corporation and the nonprofit. Thus, for example, when the Swiss pharmaceutical manufacturer Novartis contributed $25 million to the University of California at Berkeley for basic biological research, it secured in the bargain the right to negotiate licenses on a third of the discoveries of the school's Department of Plant and Microbial Biology, whether it paid for these discoveries or not.[36] Management expert Rosabeth Moss Kanter even argues that businesses are coming to see nonprofits not simply as sources of goodwill for businesses, but as the "beta site for business innovation," a locus for developing new approaches to long-standing business problems such as how to attract inner-city customers to the banking system or how to locate and train entry-level personnel for central-city hotels.[37] In these and countless other ways nonprofit organizations and businesses have begun reaching out to each other across historic divides of suspicion to forge interesting collaborations of value to both. Though not without their problems, these partnerships have led the Aspen Institute's Nonprofit Sector Strategy Group, comprised of nonprofit, academic, business, and government leaders, to "applaud the new strategic approach that businesses are bringing to societal problem-solving and the expansion of business partnerships with nonprofit groups to which it has given rise."[38]

Building a Nonprofit Infrastructure

In addition to absorbing significant aspects of the dominant market culture, nonprofit America has been busily building up its own institutional infrastructure. Fortunately, some precedent for this was established in the Charity Aid Societies formed to coordinate the work of local nonprofit organizations toward the end of the nineteenth century, and in the subsector organizations representing particular industries (for example, hospitals, higher education, museums) created in the early part of the twentieth century. But the considerable growth of this sector, its increased involvement with government, and the growing pressures for professionalization have led over the past twenty to twenty-five years to a considerable filling out of this structure and a fundamental change in its character with the emergence of a new class of infrastructure organizations devoted not to a particular nonprofit industry, but to the nonprofit sector as a whole.[39] Indeed, according to historian Peter Hall, the nonprofit sector was literally "invented" as a concept during this period.[40]

The result has been a substantial enlargement of the organizational apparatus providing services, support, and representation for the nonprofit sector as a whole. Independent Sector, the largest and most visible of the sectorwide infrastructure groups, was created in 1980 and now numbers over 700 foundations, corporations, and nonprofit umbrella organizations among its members. Other organizations have been formed to represent organized philanthropy (for example, the Council on Foundations, the Association of Small Foundations, the Forum of Regional Associations of Grantmakers), nonprofit organizations in particular states (for example, the Maryland Association of Nonprofit Organizations, the Minnesota Council of Nonprofits, and the National Council of Nonprofit Associations), and organizations serving low-income and disfranchised populations (for example, the National Committee for Responsive Philanthropy). In addition, the research and educational apparatus of the sector has filled out substantially, with nonprofit research centers established at Yale University, Johns Hopkins University, Indiana University, Harvard University, the Urban Institute, and elsewhere; nonprofit degree or certificate programs created in close to 100 colleges and universities; and more than 700 unaffiliated management support organizations offering nondegree instruction and technical assistance to nonprofit managers. To serve this expanding network of experts, professional associations have come into existence or been enlarged (for example, the Association for Research on Nonprofit Organizations and Voluntary Action, the Alliance for Nonprofit Management, the International Society for Third-Sector Research), professional journals have been launched or revamped (for example, *Nonprofit and Voluntary Sector Quarterly, Nonprofit Management and Leadership, Voluntas*); special nonprofit sections have been added to existing journals (for example, *Harvard Business Review*); and a nonprofit press created (*Chronicle of Philanthropy, Nonprofit Times, Nonprofit Quarterly*). What was once a scatteration of largely overlooked institutions has thus become a booming cottage industry attracting organizations, personnel, publications, services, conferences, websites, head-hunting firms, consultants, rituals, and fads—all premised on the proposition that nonprofit organizations are distinctive institutions with enough commonalities, despite their many differences, to be studied, represented, serviced, and trained as a group.

Meeting the For-Profit Competition

Nonprofits have also begun to demonstrate a capacity to hold their own in the face of escalating for-profit competition. This is most clearly evident in the fields of hospital and nursing home care, in both of which nonprofits have increased their relative position in recent years, as reflected in table 3-3.

To be sure, the credit for this does not belong to nonprofits alone. Rather, the for-profit sector has proved to be far less formidable a competitor in many of the spheres where both operate than initially seemed to be the case. As Bradford Gray and Mark Schlesinger argue, a "life cycle" perspective is needed to understand the competitive relationship between nonprofit and for-profit organizations in the health field, and a similar observation very likely applies to other fields as well.[41] For-profit firms have distinct advantages during growth spurts in the life cycles of particular fields, when new services are in demand as a result of changes in government policy or consumer needs. This is so because these firms can more readily access the capital markets to build new facilities, acquire new technology, and attract sophisticated management. In addition, they are better equipped to market their services and achieve the scale required to negotiate favorable terms with suppliers (for example, pharmaceutical companies). However, once they become heavily leveraged, the continued success of these enterprises comes to depend greatly on the expectation of continuing escalation of their stock prices. When this expectation is shaken, as it often has been due to shifts in government reimbursement policies under both Medicare and Medicaid, the results can be catastrophic and precipitous, producing sharp drops in stock valuations. In such circumstances, for-profit firms have shown a distressing tendency to engage in fraudulent practices. In the 1990s, for example, for-profit nursing homes, squeezed by new state policies designed to reduce Medicaid costs, turned to misleading billing practices to sustain their revenues and ultimately got caught. A similar scenario played out in the hospital field twice in the past two decades—first in the late 1980s and again in the mid-1990s—and a third episode appears to be under way as this book goes to press. In each of these cases, overly optimistic for-profit entrepreneurs found it impossible to sustain the growth paths that their stock valuations required and ended up being discredited when government agencies and private insurers charged that they had fraudulently inflated their costs and overbilled for services.[42] This boom-and-bust cycle seems to operate as well in the social service field, particularly where government support is a crucial part of the demand structure of agencies. For-profit involvement grows in response to increased public funding, but then suffers a shake-out when government reimbursement contracts.

All of this demonstrates why nonprofit involvement is so crucial, especially in fields such as health care, drug abuse prevention, hospice care, and chronic disease treatment, where the public has a crucial stake in maintaining a durable level of quality care. At the same time, such involvement is far from guaranteed, even where nonprofits pioneer the service, as has been the case in much of the health, education, social services, and arts fields. Given the intensity of competition at the present time and the expanded access of for-profits to government support, nonprofits can hold their own only where they have well-established institutions, where they can secure capital, where they manage to identify a meaningful market niche and a distinctive product, where they respond effectively to the competitive threat, and where individual consumers, or those who are paying on their behalf, value the special qualities that the nonprofits bring to the field. The fact that nonprofits have continued to expand substantially even in fields such as home health and day care in which for-profits have gained a competitive edge, and that they have held their own and even expanded their relative position in fields like nursing home care, acute care hospitals, and the arts in which for-profits were growing rapidly, suggests that many nonprofits have been up to this challenge. Recent reports about problems facing nonprofit hospitals in generating capital to respond to a surprising spurt in demand make it clear, however, that serious challenges remain.[43]

Meeting the Political Competition

Even more impressive than their ability to fend off for-profit economic competition has been the success nonprofit organizations have had in fending off for-profit political competition. This achievement is especially surprising in view of the role that money has come to play in American politics, the serious economic pressures under which nonprofit organizations are operating, and the apparent decline in civic participation identified by scholars such as Robert Putnam.[44] It is also all the more remarkable in light of the legal limitations on nonprofit political action—limitations that bar nonprofit organizations from engaging in electoral activity, from contributing to political campaigns, and from devoting more than a limited share of their resources to either direct or indirect "lobbying" (that is, attempting to influence particular pieces of legislation or administrative actions). Indeed, only 1.5 percent of all nonprofit 501(c)(3) organizations that filed the required Form 990 with the Internal Revenue Service in 1998 reported any expenditures on lobbying, and the amount they spent represented less than a tenth of 1 percent of their expenditures.[45]

Despite these limitations, however, nonprofits have amassed a quite extraordinary recent record of advocacy achievements, of identifying unmet needs and actively promoting changes in both public and private policy to address them. One manifestation of this has been the sizable number of recent social and political "movements" mentioned earlier, virtually all of which have taken form within the nation's nonprofit institutions. More generally, the past twenty to thirty years have witnessed the growing political influence of a variety of citizen groups, which mobilize members, donors, or activists around interests other than their vocation or profession. As political scientist Jeffrey Berry shows, such groups constitute at most only 7 percent of the Washington interest group universe, yet between the early 1960s and the early 1990s they accounted for anywhere from 24 to 32 percent of the testimony at congressional hearings, for between 29 and 40 percent of the press coverage of pending legislation, and for a disproportionate share of the commentary on the nightly news.[46] In the process, they managed to move their essentially nonmaterial issues to the top of the congressional agenda. What is more, this disproportionate attention ultimately translated into disproportionate policy success, as these groups were nearly 80 percent as effective in passing legislation they favored as the business lobbies against which they were often arrayed. As Berry points out:

> In every measurement taken so far, liberal citizen groups have demonstrated that they are effective and tenacious Washington lobbies. . . . Even if business remains more powerful, liberal citizen groups have proved that they are worthy adversaries capable of influencing policymakers.[47]

Not only have nonprofit citizen groups proved effective in national political advocacy, but also these organizations have recently extended their reach upward to the international level and downward to states and localities. The same new communications technologies that have

facilitated the rise of global corporations have permitted the emergence of transnational advocacy networks linking nonprofit citizen
groups across national borders. This "third force" is rapidly transforming international politics and economics, challenging government
policies on everything from land mines to dam construction and holding corporations to account in their home markets for environmental
damage or unfair labor practices they may be pursuing in far-off
lands.[48] Indeed, the recent eagerness that multinational corporations
have shown for cause-related marketing arrangements and broader
strategic partnerships with nonprofit organizations has been driven in
important part by the threat these networks pose to their "license to
operate" and to their reputations among both consumers and their
own staff. Similarly, nonprofits have forged advocacy coalitions at the
state level to make sure that devolution does not emasculate policy
gains achieved nationally. The expansion of state social welfare and
arts spending cited earlier can probably be attributed in important
part to this nonprofit policy advocacy at the state level.

That nonprofit citizen groups have been able to develop such clout
is due in part to changes in public attitudes and in political circumstances—the declining influence of political parties, the growing public concern about amenities such as clean water and air, and the end of
the cold war. But at least as important has been the capacity and effectiveness of the citizen organizations themselves—their ability to attract
resources and talented personnel, the dedication and seriousness with
which they have approached their work, and the effectiveness they
have shown in utilizing the resources at their command. Nonprofit
advocacy organizations have blossomed into highly sophisticated
organizations commanding millions of dollars of resources. The Sierra
Club, for example, has sixty-five chapters throughout the United
States, with 550,000 members, a separate Sierra Club Foundation,
and a Sierra Club Political Action Committee. The Nature Conservancy is now a holding company for five nonexempt and four exempt
organizations, including a Nature Conservancy Action Fund, and

oversees 300 state and local organizations.[49] Not only are many of these organizations large and complex, however, they also seem to be increasingly well managed. As Berry shows, these groups have built substantial donor bases, earned a reputation for doing their homework, and consequentl' enjoy at least as much credibility as their corporate, trade, or prof ssional association opponents.[50]

6

Resetting the Balance:
The Task Ahead

Nonprofit America has thus responded with extraordinary creativity and resilience to the challenges and opportunities it has confronted over the past twenty years. The sector has grown enormously as a consequence—in numbers, in revenues, and in the range of purposes it serves. In addition, it seems to have expanded its competencies and improved its management, though these are more difficult to gauge with precision. To be sure, not all components of the sector have experienced these changes to the same degree or even in the same direction. Yet what is striking is how widespread the adaptations seem to have been.

In large part, what allowed nonprofit organizations not only to survive but also to thrive during this period was that they moved, often decisively, toward the market. Nonprofit organizations took active advantage of the growing demand for their services, expanded their fee income, launched commercial ventures, forged partnerships with businesses, adopted business-style management techniques, mastered new consumer-side forms of government funding, reshaped their organizational structures, incorporated sophisticated marketing and money-management techniques into even their charitable fund-raising, and generally found new ways to tap the dynamism and resources of the market to promote their organizational objectives. This move toward the market has by no means been universal. Nor is it entirely new. What is more, it did not exhaust the range of responses the sector made to the challenges it faced. Yet it has clearly been the dominant theme of the 1990s and into the new century and its scope and impact have been profound, affecting all parts of the sector to some extent. As a result, the nonprofit sector that has entered the twenty-first century is not "your father's nonprofit sector." Rather, it has been substantially re-engineered, and this process is still very much under way, though it has yet to be fully appreciated by the sector itself or by the nation at large.

On balance, these changes seem to have worked to the advantage of the nonprofit sector, strengthening its fiscal base, upgrading its operations, enlisting new partners and new resources in its activities, and generally improving its reputation for effectiveness. But the changes have also brought significant risks, and the risks may well overwhelm the gains. Before drawing the final balance sheet on the state of nonprofit America, therefore, it is necessary to weigh the gains against these risks. It will then be possible to determine what can be done to improve the balance between risks and gains for the years ahead.

The Risks

More specifically, the nonprofit sector's response to the challenges of the past twenty years, creative as it has been, has exposed the sector to at least five important risks.

Growing Identity Crisis

In the first place, nonprofit America is confronting an identity crisis as a result of a growing tension between the market character of the services it is providing and the continued nonprofit character of the institutions providing them. This tension has become especially stark in the health field, where third-party payers, such as Medicare and private HMOs, increasingly downplay values other than actual service cost in setting reimbursement rates; where bond-rating agencies discount community service in determining the economic worth of bond issues, and hence the price that nonprofit hospitals have to pay for capital; and where fierce for-profit competition leaves little room for the conscious pursuit of social goals.[1] Left to their own devices, nonprofit institutions have had little choice but to adjust to these pressures, but at some cost to the features that make them distinctive. Under these circumstances, it is no wonder that scholars have been finding it so difficult to detect real differences between the performance of for-profit and nonprofit hospitals, and that many nonprofit HMOs and hospitals have willingly surrendered the nonprofit form or sold out to for-profit firms.[2]

Private universities are similarly experiencing increasing strains between their mission to propagate knowledge and the expansion of their reliance on corporate sponsorship, which has brought with it demands for exclusive patent rights to the fruits of university research.[3] Marketing pressures are also intruding on the operations of nonprofit arts and cultural institutions, limiting their ability to focus on artistic quality, and transforming them, as Margaret Wyszomirski notes, into social enterprises more attentive to market demands.[4] So intense has the resulting identity crisis become, in fact, that some scholars are beginning to reject the long-standing notion that nonprofits are reluctant participants in the market, providing only those "private goods" needed to support their "collective goods" activities, and are coming to see many of them functioning instead as essentially commercial operations, dominated by "pecuniary rather than altruistic objectives."[5]

Increased Demands on Nonprofit Managers

These tensions have naturally complicated the job of the nonprofit executive, requiring these officials to master not only the substantive dimensions of their fields, but also the broader private markets within which they operate, the numerous public policies that affect them, and the massive new developments in technology and management with which they must contend. They must do all this, moreover, while balancing an increasingly complex array of stakeholders that includes not only clients, staff, board members, and private donors, but also regulators, government program officials, for-profit competitors, and business partners; and while also demonstrating performance and competing with other nonprofits and with for-profit firms for fees, board members, customers, contracts, grants, donations, gifts, bequests, visibility, prestige, political influence, and volunteers.[6] No wonder that executive burn-out has become such a serious problem in the field, despite the excitement and fulfillment the role entails.

Increased Threat to Nonprofit Missions

Inevitably, these pressures pose threats to the continued pursuit of nonprofit missions. Nonprofit organizations forced to rely on fees and charges naturally begin to skew their service offerings to clientele who are able to pay. What start out as sliding fee scales designed to cross-subsidize services for the needy become core revenue sources essential for agency survival. Organizations needing to raise capital to expand are naturally tempted to locate new facilities in places with a client base able to finance the borrowing costs. When charity care, advocacy, and research are not covered in government or private reimbursement rates, institutions have little choice but to curtail these activities.

How far these pressures have proceeded is difficult to say with any precision. As William Diaz has observed, support for the poor has never been the exclusive, or the primary, focus of nonprofit action.[7] Nor need it be. What is more, many of the developments identified here have usefully mobilized market resources to support genuinely charitable purposes. Yet the nonprofit sector's movement toward the market is creating significant pressures to move away from those in greatest need, to focus on amenities that appeal to those who can pay, and to apply the market test to all facets of organizational operations.[8]

The move to the market may thus be posing a far greater threat to the nonprofit sector's historic social justice and civic mission than the growth of government support before it.

Disadvantaging Small Agencies

A fourth risk resulting from the nonprofit sector's recent move to the market is to put smaller agencies at an increasing disadvantage. Successful adaptation to the prevailing market pressures requires access to advanced technology, professional marketing, corporate partners, sophisticated fundraising, and complex government reimbursement systems, all of which are problematic for smaller agencies. Market pressures are therefore creating not just a digital divide, but a much broader "sustainability chasm" that smaller organizations are finding increasingly difficult to bridge. Although such agencies can cope with these pressures in part through collaborations and partnerships, these devices themselves often require sophisticated management and absorb precious managerial energies.[9] As the barriers to entry, and particularly to sustainability, rise, the nonprofit sector is thus at risk of losing some of its most precious qualities—its ease of entry and its availability as a testing ground for new ideas.

Potential Loss of Public Trust

All of this, finally, poses a further threat to the public trust on which the nonprofit sector ultimately depends. Thanks to the pressures they are under, and the agility they have shown in response to them, American nonprofit organizations have moved well beyond the quaint, Norman Rockwell stereotype of selfless volunteers ministering to the needy and supported largely by charitable gifts. Yet popular and media images remain wedded to this older image, and far too little attention has been given to bringing popular perceptions into better alignment with the realities that now exist, and to justifying these realities to a skeptical citizenry and press. As a consequence, nonprofits find themselves vulnerable when highly visible events, such as the September 11 tragedy, let alone instances of mismanagement or scandal, reveal them to be far more complex and commercially engaged institutions than the public suspects.

The more successfully nonprofit organizations respond to the dominant market pressures, therefore, the greater the risk they face of sacrificing the public trust on which they ultimately depend. This may help explain part of the appeal of the Bush administration's "faith-based charities" initiative. What makes this concept so appealing is its comforting affirmation of the older image of the nonprofit sector, the image of voluntary church groups staffed by the faithful solving the nation's problems of poverty and blight, even though, as noted earlier, this image grossly exaggerates both the capacity and the inclinations of most congregations to engage in meaningful social problem solving.

The Task Ahead

What all of this suggests is that a better balance may need to be struck between what Bradford Gray and Mark Schlesinger term the nonprofit sector's "distinctiveness imperative," that is, the things that make nonprofits special; and the sector's "survival imperative," that is, the things nonprofits need to do in order to survive.[10] To be sure, these two imperatives are not wholly in conflict. Nevertheless, the tensions between them are real and there is increasing reason to worry that the survival imperative may be gaining the upper hand. To correct this, steps will be needed in both domains, and the steps will require support from many different quarters.

The Distinctiveness Imperative

Actions to address the nonprofit sector's distinctiveness imperative are perhaps the most urgent. Recent research confirms that what attracts people to nonprofit organizations to work and volunteer is the opportunity these organizations provide to help the public, to do something worthwhile, and to make a difference.[11] These sentiments have grown increasingly important as well to other segments of the work force, as the growing corporate attention to social responsibility attests. In the wake of recent scandals that have tarnished the image of corporate America, the dangers of too hasty a nonprofit embrace of the market and too easy a surrender of nonprofit distinctiveness have become especially apparent. To avoid this, several types of action are needed.

RETHINKING COMMUNITY BENEFIT AND CHARITABLE PURPOSE. In the first place, action is needed in the realm of values and ideas. In a sense, nonprofit organizations have been so busy coping with the powerful market forces they are facing that they have allowed the market definitions of value to dominate the public discourse and even their own behavior. Largely lacking, as the *Nonprofit Quarterly* recently noted, is "agreement around a powerful affirmation of identity distinguishing [the nonprofit sector] from the other two social sectors."[12] To the extent that any consensus exists on this point as reflected in court decisions, legislative proposals, and popular accounts, it focuses on care for the poor as the chief, or exclusive, rationale for nonprofit status. But this is far too narrow a ground for the sector to defend successfully given the survival demands it also confronts and the other functions it performs. Nonprofits must therefore develop a broader and more coherent statement of "the nature of [their] game."[13] This will require a serious rethinking of the central concepts of charitable purpose and community benefit that justify the nonprofit sector's existence. As Aspen Institute scholars Alan Abramson and Rachel McCarthy have pointed out, this is a task for which the nonprofit infrastructure organizations are especially suited, but not one they have yet effectively addressed.[14]

Illustrative of the direction this might take is the suggestion by Gray and Schlesinger to extend the concept of community benefit for nonprofit hospitals to embrace not only charity care but a broader commitment to community health and to the production of collective goods such as trained medical professionals and scientific advance.[15]

Similar insights can be found in Forman and Stoddard's discussion of the recent efforts of nonprofit humanitarian assistance agencies to forge new principles of humanitarian aid that take account of the complex humanitarian/military crises increasingly common around the world.[16] More generally, nonprofit America must give broader and more concrete meaning to its claims to serve the public good by stressing the sector's commitments to reliability, to trustworthiness, to quality, to equity, to community, and to individual and community empowerment. These are powerful rationales in a society that values pluralism and freedom but wishes to balance them with a sense of solidarity and responsibility for others. But they must be more forcefully and concretely articulated and then be more fully interpreted and applied in the context of particular agencies and fields.

IMPROVING PUBLIC UNDERSTANDING. As efforts go forward to clarify the nonprofit sector's vision and rationale, parallel efforts must be made to communicate this vision to the public and reconcile it with how the sector actually works. This must go beyond the ritualistic celebrations of charitable giving and voluntarism that currently form the heart of the sector's public relations effort, important though these may be. Rather, the public must be introduced to the broader realities of current nonprofit operations, to the remarkable resilience that the sector has shown in recent years, and to the full range of special qualities that make nonprofit organizations worth protecting. This will require a better public defense of the sector's long-standing partnership with government, clarification of the special ways in which nonprofits are enlisting market means to promote nonprofit ends, and the further development and dissemination of codes of conduct to help nonprofits and the public understand the delicate balance nonprofits have to strike between their survival and distinctiveness needs.

POLICY SHIFTS. Changes may also be needed in public policy to make sure that the nonprofit sector's commitments to community benefit

and charitable purpose are given effective incentives and are rein-
forced. This may require challenging the narrow conceptions of charitable purpose embodied in some legal opinions. But it may also
require some tightening of the legal provisions under which nonprofits
operate. At a minimum, this could involve more stringent policing of
the existing "unrelated business income" tax provisions to ensure that
nonprofit organizations pay income taxes on business activities that
stray too far from their charitable purposes. Beyond this, it could
involve shifting from the current system of tax-exempt *organizations* to
a system of tax-exempt *activities,* under which organizations would
earn exemptions from taxes only for those activities that support valid
public, or community, purposes. Under such a system, nonprofit
organizations would have to justify their exemptions in annual tax fil-
ings that identify the share of their income that goes to support such
purposes. Such a system would provide more regular reinforcement of
the community benefits nonprofits are supposed to provide and help
reassure the public that these benefits are being provided.

The Survival Imperative

For this effort to promote the "distinctiveness imperative" of nonprofit
organizations to work, however, steps are also needed to ease the survival imperative under which these organizations labor. As we have
seen, these survival pressures have grown increasingly intense in recent
years, putting pursuit of the sector's charitable missions increasingly at
risk. To free nonprofits to attend to their distinctive roles in this
increasingly competitive environment, special steps are therefore
needed. Three of these deserve particular mention here.

CAPITALIZING THE SECTOR. In the first place, additional steps are
needed to correct the structural impediments that nonprofit organizations face in generating investment capital because of their lack of
access to the equity markets. More than any other single cause, these
impediments explain the difficulty nonprofit organizations have faced

in responding to technological change and maintaining their market niche during periods of rapid expansion of demand. The experience of nonprofit hospitals and higher education institutions demonstrates, however, that nonprofit organizations can often hold their own in such circumstances when they can gain access to the needed capital at competitive rates. In both of these cases, special tax incentives were provided to subsidize bonds issued to finance nonprofit facilities. The recent example of nonprofit involvement in low-income housing tells a similar story in a context characterized by smaller-scale institutions. Here the provision of special tax advantages for investors was supplemented by the emergence of nonprofit intermediary institutions that package the tax breaks for sale to investors and then distribute the proceeds to smaller, community-based organizations.

Many nonprofit organizations, particularly in the human services field, still lack access to such tax breaks and the capital funds these tax breaks can leverage, however. As a consequence, they are at a competitive disadvantage in keeping up with rapid technological change and meeting increased demand. What is more, the existing incentives available to nonprofit hospitals and education institutions have lost some of their value as a result of recent tax law changes that have reduced the taxation of dividends, since these changes will decrease the relative attractiveness of tax-exempt bonds to investors.

To correct this, a broader nonprofit investment tax credit could usefully be enacted. Such a measure would create a more level playing field for nonprofit agencies, ease the survival pressures they face, and thus better enable them to continue performing their distinctive roles.

BUY-IN BY THIRD-PARTY PAYERS. By itself, improved access to capital for nonprofit organizations will still not give nonprofits the financial leeway they need to address their distinctive missions unless steps are also taken to relieve the fiscal squeeze these organizations face. That squeeze, in turn, is increasingly shaped by the reimbursement policies

of third-party payers—private insurance companies, health maintenance organizations, corporate benefit administrators, and government
voucher programs like Medicare and Medicaid. Whether nonprofit
hospitals can continue to support their teaching and research functions, for example, is significantly affected by whether Medicare con-
siders this function vital enough to justify an adjustment in the nor-
mal hospital reimbursement rate.

Increasingly, third-party payers have been ratcheting down the
kinds of functions they are willing to support in this way, requiring
the providers of health care, clinic care, nursing home care, drug abuse
treatment, day care, foster care, and many other services to shave costs
to the bone, often at the expense of mission-critical functions such as
advocacy, community organizing, and care for the poor. To reverse this
trend, nonprofit organizations will have to convince third-party payers
that these activities are both worthy of support and able to be supported. The recent decision of Blue Shield of California to adopt an
incentive system that takes account of quality, and not just cost, in setting hospital reimbursement rates is promising in this regard, but there
clearly is still a long way to go.[17]

ENCOURAGEMENT OF PRIVATE GIVING. The nonprofit survival imperative can also be eased through continued and expanded encouragement of charitable giving and volunteering, particularly that targeted
on community benefit activities. While this source cannot realistically
be counted on to provide a major share of nonprofit income, it nevertheless offers an important extra edge in sustaining mission and connecting the sector to its popular base and to its fundamental values.

Given the recent string of policy changes working against the
growth of charitable giving,[18] it seems clear that something dramatic
may be needed just to stem the steady decline in giving's share of total
nonprofit income. One such possibility would be to replace the existing tax deduction system with one based on tax "credits." Unlike

deductions, which deliver more tax benefits per dollar of contribution to upper-income taxpayers than to lower-income ones, tax credits provide the same tax benefits to all taxpayers, regardless of their income.[19] What is more, the scale of the credits can be geared to the particular community benefits being promoted simply by varying the share of the contribution that can be used to offset taxes for various types of contributions. American charitable giving has been stuck below 2 percent of personal income for some time. It is worth considering radical approaches that might boost this level in the future, and a system of tax credits instead of deductions might well be one of those worth trying.

Conclusion

It has been said that the quality of a nation can be seen in the way it treats its least advantaged citizens. But it can also be seen in the way it treats its most valued institutions. Americans have long paid lip service to the importance they attach to their voluntary institutions, while largely ignoring the challenges these institutions face. During the past two decades, these challenges have been extraordinary. But so, too, has been the nonprofit sector's response. As a result, the state of nonprofit America is surprisingly robust as we enter the new millennium, with more organizations doing more things more effectively than ever before.

At the same time, the movement to the market that has made this possible has also exposed the sector to enormous risks. What is more, the risks go to the heart of what makes the nonprofit sector distinctive and worthy of public support—its basic identity, its mission, and its ability to retain the public's trust.

Up to now, nonprofit managers have had to fend for themselves in deciding what risks it was acceptable to take in order to permit their organizations to survive. Given the stake that American society has in the preservation of these institutions and in the protection of their ability to perform their distinctive roles, it seems clear that this must now change. Americans need to rethink in a more explicit way whether the balance between survival and distinctiveness that nonprofit institutions have had to strike in recent years is the right one for the future, and if not, what steps might now be needed to shift this balance for the years ahead.

The argument here is that some such adjustments are needed, that America's nonprofit institutions require broader support in preserving the features that make them special. Whether others agree with this conclusion remains to be seen. What seems clear, however, is that better public understanding of the state of nonprofit America is needed if such judgments are to be possible. My hope is that this book will contribute to such understanding.

Notes

Chapter 1

1. Gilbert M. Gaul and May Pat Flaherty, "Red Cross Collected Unneeded Blood: Resources Lacking to Freeze Surplus," *Washington Post,* November 11, 2001, p. A1.

2. AAFRC Trust for Philanthropy, "What Do Crises Mean for Philanthropy," *Giving USA Update,* no. 4 (2001), p. 3.

3. For a useful discussion of some of these dilemmas, see C. Eugene Steuerle, "Managing Charitable Giving in the Wake of Disaster," and Victoria B. Bjorklund, "Reflections on September 11: Legal Developments," in *September 11: Perspectives from the Field of Philanthropy* (New York: Foundation Center, 2002), pp. 1–10, 11–46.

4. For a discussion of this partnership, see Lester M. Salamon, "Partners in Public Service," in Walter W. Powell, ed., *The Nonprofit Sector: A Research Handbook* (Yale University Press, 1987), pp. 99–117; and Lester M. Salamon, *Partners in Public Service: Government-Nonprofit Relations in the Modern Welfare State* (Johns Hopkins University Press, 1995).

5. Alexis de Tocqueville, *Democracy in America,* vol. II, the Henry Reeve Text, as revised by Francis Bowen (Vintage Books, [1835] 1945), p. 118.

6. For the full results of this larger project, see Lester M. Salamon, ed., *The State of Nonprofit America* (Brookings, 2002). The present book originally

appeared in somewhat abridged form as chapter 1 of this broader volume, though it has been updated here.

7. On the re-engineering movement in the corporate sector, see Michael Hammer and James Champy, *Reengineering the Corporation: A Manifesto for Business Revolution,* rev. ed. (London: Nicholas Brealey Publishing, 1994); Michael Hammer and James Champy, *Reengineering the Corporation: A Manifesto for Business Revolution* (London: Nicholas Brealy Publishing, 1993); David K. Carr and Henry J. Johnson. *Best Practices in Reengineering: What Works and What Doesn't in the Reengineering Process* (McGraw-Hill, 1995).

8. See, for example, Kevin P. Kearns, *Private Sector Strategies for Social Sector Success: The Guide to Strategy and Planning for Pubic and Nonprofit Organizations* (San Francisco: Jossey-Bass, 2000).

Chapter 2

1. For a fuller discussion of the legal definition of a "nonprofit organization," see Bruce R. Hopkins, *The Law of Tax-Exempt Organizations,* 7th ed. (John Wiley, 1998), pp. 3–23. See also Lester M. Salamon, *America's Nonprofit Sector: A Primer,* 2d ed. (New York: Foundation Center, 1999), pp. 7–11.

2. Section 501(c)(4) organizations share these basic purposes but are permitted to pursue them more extensively through "lobbying" efforts, something 501(c)(3) organizations can do only to a limited extent. Because of this, contributions to the 501c(4) organizations are not tax deductible, although the organizations themselves are tax exempt. This distinction between 501(c)(3) and 501(c)(4) organizations is a notoriously slippery one, depending on the definition of the term "lobbying" and the extent of the restriction on the 501c(3) organizations not to engage in it to a "substantial" extent. Recent laws have attempted to clarify this distinction by specifying more precisely what falls within the domain of lobbying and what exactly is meant by "substantial." Fundamentally, lobbying means direct or indirect efforts to influence the passage of particular pieces of legislation or particular administrative rules; while "substantial" has come to mean roughly 20 percent or more of agency expenditures. In addition to sections 501(c)(3) and 501(c)(4), the U.S. tax code contains over twenty other subsections under which organizations can be granted tax exemptions. These include business associations, labor unions, and social clubs. None of these types of organizations is eligible to receive tax deductible gifts, however, because they are member serving rather than public serving. See Hopkins, *The Law of Tax-Exempt Organizations.*

3. Based on data presented in Salamon, *America's Nonprofit Sector,* pp. 22 and 41, n. 2. Religious congregations are not required to register for tax-exempt status, though many do.

4. Murray S. Weitzman and others, *The New Nonprofit Almanac and Desk Reference* (San Francisco: Jossey-Bass, 2002), p. 21.

5. U.S. Census Bureau, *Statistical Abstract of the United States, 2000,* 120th ed. (Government Printing Office, 2000), p. 420.

6. Virginia B. Hodgkinson and Murray S. Weitzman, *Nonprofit Almanac: 1996/1997* (San Francisco: Jossey-Bass, 1996), pp. 271–309.

7. Weitzman and others, *New Nonprofit Almanac,* p. 125. See also Internal Revenue Service, *Statistics of Income Bulletin,* Publication 1136 (February 1997), table 21.

8. Elizabeth Boris, "The Nonprofit Sector in the 1990s," in Charles T. Clotfelter and Thomas Ehrlich, eds., *Philanthropy and the Nonprofit Sector in a Changing America* (Indiana University Press, 1999), pp. 16–17.

9. The discussion here draws heavily on Salamon, *America's Nonprofit Sector,* pp. 15–17 and below.

10. See, for example, James S. Coleman, *Foundations of Social Theory* (Harvard University Press, 1990), pp. 300–21; Robert Putnam, *Making Democracy Work: Civic Traditions in Modern Italy* (Princeton University Press, 1993), pp. 83–116, 163–85.

11. Alexis de Tocqueville, *Democracy in America,* vol. II, the Henry Reeve Text, as revised by Francis Bowen (Vintage Books, [1835] 1945), p. 117.

12. The term *value guardian* was first used by Ralph Kramer to describe the crucial role nonprofit organizations play in promoting the tradition of volunteering, but it has a broader meaning as well. Ralph Kramer, *Voluntary Agencies in the Welfare State* (University of California Press, 1981), pp. 193–211.

Chapter 3

1. For example, Harvard College, the first nonprofit, was financed in important part by an earmarked tax on corn levied by the colonial government of Massachusetts, beginning in the seventeenth century. Similarly, subsidies for nonprofit human service provision were a standard feature of American urban life in the 1880s and 1890s. By the mid-1890s, in fact, more government welfare aid in New York, Pennsylvania, Connecticut, Maryland, and even the District of Columbia went to support private institutions than public ones, and far more of the income of private nonprofit organizations in a wide variety of fields came from government than from private philanthropy. One early study showed, for example, that in New

York City, 69 percent of the income of a group of prominent nonprofit children's agencies came from public subsidies. On higher education, see John S. Whitehead. *The Separation of College and State: Columbia, Dartmouth, Harvard, and Yale* (Yale University Press, 1973), pp. 3–16; on social services, see Amos Warner, *American Charities: A Study in Philanthropy and Economics* (New York: Thomas Y. Crowell, 1894), pp. 400–05.

For a more complete analysis of this system of government-nonprofit relations and the broader pattern of "third-party government" of which it is a part, see Lester M. Salamon, "Partners in Public Service," in Walter W. Powell, ed., *The Nonprofit Sector: A Research Handbook* (Yale University Press, 1987), pp. 99–117; and Lester M. Salamon, *Partners in Public Service: Government-Nonprofit Relations in the Modern Welfare State* (Johns Hopkins University Press, 1995). For a discussion of the federal government's support of nonprofit research universities in the 1940s and 1950s, see Don K. Price, *The Scientific Estate* (Harvard University Press, 1965).

2. Lester M. Salamon and Alan J. Abramson, "The Federal Budget and the Nonprofit Sector: Implications of the *Contract with America*," in Dwight F. Burlingame, William A. Diaz, Warren F. Ilchman and Associates, *Capacity for Change? The Nonprofit World in the Age of Devolution* (Indiana University Center on Philanthropy, 1996), pp. 8–9; Alan J. Abramson, Lester M. Salamon, and C. Eugene Steurle, "The Nonprofit Sector and the Federal Budget: Recent History and Future Directions," in Elizabeth T. Boris and C. Eugene Steurle, eds. *Nonprofits and Government: Collaboration and Conflict* (Washington: Urban Institute Press, 1999), pp. 110–12.

3. "David Rosenbaum, "Bush Plans Little More Money for Bulk of Federal Programs," *New York Times,* January 22, 2003, p. A19; Edmund L. Andrews, "Data Show Rapid Growth in Federal Budget Shortfall," *New York Times,* January 25, 2003, p. A12.

4. Jodi Wilgoren, "New Governors Discover the Ink Is Turning Redder," *New York Times,* January 14, 2003, p. A20; David A. Rosenaum, "States Make Cuts and Increase Fees as Revenues Drop," *New York Times,* May 16, 2002, p. A1; Jodi Wilgoren, "As Deadline Nears, 9 States are Stalled in Budget Discord," *New York Times,* June 27, 2003, p. A1.

5. Office of Management and Budget, *Enhancing Governmental Productivity through Competition: A New Way of Doing Business within the Government to Provide Quality Government at Least Cost,* p. 15, quoted in Donald Kettl, *Shared Power: Public Governance and Private Markets* (Brookings, 1993), p. 46.

6. Vouchers essentially provide targeted assistance to eligible recipients in the form of a certificate or a reimbursement card that can be presented to the

provider of choice. The provider then receives payment for the certificate or reimbursement from the government. Tax expenditures use a similar method, except that no actual certificate is used. Rather, eligible taxpayers are allowed to deduct a given proportion of the cost of a particular service (for example, day care) either from their income (tax deduction) or from the taxes they owe (tax credit). For a discussion of vouchers, tax expenditures, and other tools of public action, as well as the general trend toward more indirect forms of public action, see Lester M. Salamon, ed., *The Tools of Government: A Guide to the New Governance* (Oxford University Press, 2002).

7. Medicare is a direct federal program financing health care for the elderly. Medicaid is a federal-state program financing health care and related services for the poor. Both operate through essentially voucher-type reimbursement arrangements in which clients receive services from the vendors of their choice and government essentially reimburses the vendors, initially on the basis of cost, and more recently on the basis of a pre-fixed amount.

8. Salamon, *Partners in Public Service*, p. 208.

9. Spending on Medicaid, for example, swelled more than four-fold in real dollar terms between 1975 and 1998, while discretionary spending stagnated or declined. Computed from data in U.S. House of Representatives, Committee on Ways and Means, *2000 Green Book: Background Material and Data on Programs within the Jurisdiction of the Committee on Ways and Means,* 106th Cong. 2d sess. (October 6, 2000), pp. 912, 923.

10. House Committee on Ways and Means, *2000 Green Book*, pp. 599, 617.

11. Funding for the Social Service Block Grant Program, which funds a wide array of social services and not just day care, declined, in nominal dollars, from $2.8 billion in the early 1990s to $1.8 billion in 2000. House Committee on Ways and Means, *2000 Green Book*, p. 634.

12. Bradford H. Gray and Mark Schlesinger, "Health," in Lester M. Salamon, ed., *The State of Nonprofit America* (Brookings, 2002), pp. 74–75; Stephen R. Smith, "Social Services," in Salamon, *The State of Nonprofit America*, pp. 174–77.

13. Of these, 40 percent of the large-establishment employees and 35 percent of the small-establishment employees were covered by "preferred provider" plans, and the balance by true health maintenance organizations (HMOs). U.S. Census Bureau, *Statistical Abstract of the United States, 2000,* 120th ed. (Government Printing Office, 2000), table 180, p. 119.

14. A recent survey of American congregations found that most congregations are quite small, with annual budgets averaging $55,000. Most have no more than one full-time paid staff position, and 40 percent do not have even this. Only 6 percent of congregations have a staff person devoting at least a

quarter time to social service projects. Summarizing these data, analyst Mark Chaves notes: "the vast majority of congregational resources are spent producing religion and maintaining the congregation itself, not providing social services to a broader community." Mark Chaves, "Religious Congregations," in Salamon, *The State of Nonprofit America,* pp. 278, 283, 289.

15. Author's estimates based on data in Murray S. Weitzman and others, *The New Nonprofit Almanac and Desk Reference* (San Francisco: Jossey-Bass, 2002), pp. 96–97.

16. For further detail, see Virginia Hodgkinson, with Kathryn Nelson and Edward D. Sivak Jr., "Individual Giving and Volunteering," in Salamon, *The State of Nonprofit America,* p. 394. Generally speaking, the higher the rate of tax, the lower the out-of-pocket "cost" of a gift, since the taxpayer would have to pay more to Uncle Sam if he or she chose not to give. Paradoxically, therefore, higher tax rates increase the financial incentive to give and lower tax rates reduce this incentive.

17. See, for example, David Streitfeld, "Donations Dried up with Tech Stocks," *Los Angeles Times,* October 13, 2002, p. 1.

18. AAFRC Trust for Philanthropy, *Giving USA 2000* (Indianapolis, 2002), p. 170.

19. Computed from data in Weitzman and others, *The New Nonprofit Almanac,* pp. 96–97. These figures exclude giving to religious organizations for religious purposes but include the portion of religious giving that goes to support other charitable purposes, such as social welfare and education. With all religious giving included, the decline in giving's total share of sector income was slightly less pronounced—from 27 percent in 1977 to 20 percent in 1997.

20. The Fidelity Gift Fund recorded assets of $2.2 billion as of early 2000 and made grants of $374 million in the 1998–99 fiscal year. By comparison, the New York Community Trust reported assets of $2.0 billion as of the end of 1999 and grants during 1999 of $130.7 million. AAFRC Trust for Philanthropy, *Giving USA, 2001* (Indianapolis, 2001), p. 53; Steven Lawrence, Robin Gluck, and Dia Ganguly, *Foundation Yearbook 2001* (New York: Foundation Center, 2000), pp. 67–68. For further information, see Hodgkinson, "Individual Giving and Volunteering," pp. 400–01.

21. See, for example, Gray and Schlesinger, "Health," pp. 74–75.

22. For example, when the federal government in mid-1980 discontinued the program it had enacted in the 1970s to provide start-up capital for nonprofit health maintenance organizations, it made it difficult for nonprofit HMOs to respond to the increased demand that occurred during this period. As a result, the for-profit share of the HMO industry surged and the nonprofit share fell off. Gray and Schlesinger, "Health," p. 85.

23. William P. Ryan, "The New Landscape for Nonprofits," *Harvard Business Review* (January–February 1999), p. 128.

24. Henry Hansmann, "The Role of Nonprofit Enterprise," *Yale Law Journal*, vol. 89, no. 5 (1980), pp. 835–901.

25. See, for example, Michael Porter and Mark R. Kramer, "Philanthropy's New Agenda: Creating Value," *Harvard Business Review* (November–December 1999), pp. 121–30; Gar Walker and Jean Grossman, "Philanthropy and Outcomes," in Charles T. Clotfelter and Thomas Ehrlich, eds., *Philanthropy and the Nonprofit Sector in a Changing America* (Indiana University Press, 1999), pp. 449–60.

26. Christine W. Letts, William Ryan, and Allen Grossman, "Virtuous Capital: What Foundations Can Learn from Venture Capitalists," *Harvard Business Review* (March/April 1997), pp. 2–7.

27. H. George Frederickson, "First, There's Theory, Then There's Practice," *Foundation News and Commentary* (March/April 2001), p. 38. See also Doug Easterling, "Using Outcome Evaluation to Guide Grant Making: Theory, Reality, and Possibilities," *Nonprofit and Voluntary Sector Quarterly*, vol. 29, no. 3 (September 2000), pp. 482–86; Walker and Grossman, "Philanthropy and Outcomes."

28. Jeffrey Berry, *The New Liberalism: The Rising Power of Citizen Groups* (Brookings, 1999), esp. pp. 120–30.

29. Nicole Wallace, "Online Giving Soars as Donors Turn to the Internet Following Attacks," *Chronicle of Philanthropy*, October 4, 2001, p. 22.

30. See Atul Dighe, "Demographic and Technological Imperatives," in Salamon, *The State of Nonprofit America*, pp. 507–11.

31. See, for example, Margaret J. Wyszomirski, "Arts and Culture," in Salamon, *The State of Nonprofit America*, pp. 198–202.

32. Andrew Blau, *More Than Bit Players: How Information Technology Will Change the Ways Nonprofits and Foundations Work and Thrive in the Information Age* (New York: Surdna Foundation, May 2001), p. 10.

33. A recent survey by the Association of Arts Agencies showed, for example, that 34 percent of arts organizations had only one or no computer and 46 percent had no website. Wyszomirski, "Arts and Culture," p. 200. See, more generally, Stephen Greene, "Astride the Digital Divide: Many Charities Struggle to Make Effective Use of New Technology," *Chronicle of Philanthropy*, January 11, 2001, p. 1.

34. Blau, *More Than Bit Players*, p. 9.

35. Wyszomirski, "Arts and Culture," pp. 198–202.

36. Edwin Feulner, "Truth in Testimony," Heritage Foundation, August 22, 1996.

37. Capital Research Center, "Our Mission," November 1996, available on the website of the Capital Reseach Center.

38. Roy Lubove, *The Professional Altruist* (Harvard University Press, 1965).

39. John McKnight, *The Careless Society: Community and Its Counterfeits* (Basic Books, 1995), p. 10.

40. Stuart Butler, *Privatizing Federal Spending* (New York: Universe Books, 1985); Martin Anderson, *Imposters in the Temple: American Intellectuals Are Destroying Our Universities and Cheating Our Students* (Simon and Schuster, 1992).

41. Independent Sector, *Giving and Volunteering, 1999* (Washington, 1999), chap. 3, pp. 3, 5.

42. Jacqueline L. Salmon, "Nonprofits Show Losses in the Public's Trust," *Washington Post,* September 9, 2002, p. A2.

43. Similar evidence of public ambivalence emerges from a survey conducted for the Maryland Association of Nonprofit Organizations. Only 38 percent of the respondents in this survey indicated that they think private charitable organizations are "very trustworthy," only 29 percent "strongly agree" that the money they donate to charities is being used as they expect it to be, and 87 percent expressed worry that they are being "scammed" by telephone solicitations. Maryland Association of Nonprofit Organizations, *Protecting the Public Trust: Revisiting Attitudes about Charities in Maryland* (Baltimore, 2002).

44. Paul Light, "The Content of Their Character: The State of the Nonprofit Workforce," *Nonprofit Quarterly* (Fall 2002), p. 8.

45. Phillip Howe and Corinne McDonald, "Traumatic Stress, Turnover and Peer Support in Child Welfare," Child Welfare League of America (www.cwla.org/programs/trieschman/2001fbwPhilHowe.htm).

46. Shepard Forman and Abby Stoddard, "International Assistance," in Salamon, *The State of Nonprofit America,* pp. 257–59.

47. Lester M. Salamon and Sarah Dewees, "In Search of the Nonprofit Sector," *American Behavioral Scientist,* vol. 45, no. 11, (July 2002), pp. 1735–37; Lester M. Salamon, "What Nonprofit Wage Gap?" *Nonprofit Quarterly* (Winter 2002), pp. 61–62.

48. Thus, among public policy program graduates in the classes of 1973, 1974, 1978, and 1979, an average of 14 percent took their first jobs in the nonprofit sector and 14 percent remained employed in the nonprofit sector in the mid-1990s. By contrast, an average of 16 percent of these graduates took their first job in the private business sector and 33 percent were employed in the business sector as of the mid-1990s. Computed from data in

Paul Light, *Making Nonprofits Work: A Report on the Tides of Nonprofit Management Reform* (Brookings, 2000), p. 10.

49. Jeanne Peters, and Timothy Wolfred, *Daring to Lead: Nonprofit Executive Directors and Their Work Experience* (San Francisco: CompassPoint Nonprofit Services, August 2001), pp. 13–14, 20–21.

50. Wyszomirski, "Arts and Culture," p. 193.

51. Jeanne Peters and others, *Help Wanted: Turnover and Vacancy in Nonprofits* (San Francisco: CompassPoint Nonprofit Services, January 2002), pp. 7–8.

Chapter 4

1. The discussion here draws heavily on Lester M. Salamon, *America's Nonprofit Sector: A Primer,* 2d ed. (New York: The Foundation Center, 1999), pp. 161–67.

2. U.S. Census Bureau, *Statistical Abstract of the United States, 2000*, 120th ed. (Government Printing Office, 2000), pp. 408–09.

3. *Statistical Abstract of the United States, 2000*, table 144, p. 101.

4. 1960 and 1980 figures from U.S. Census Bureau, *Statistical Abstract of the United States, 1982/3* (GPO, 1983), table 97, p. 66; figures for 1990s from *Statistical Abstract of the United States, 2000*, table 88, p. 71.

5. U.S. House of Representatives, Committee on Ways and Means, *2000 Green Book: Background Material and Data on Programs within the Jurisdiction of the Committee on Ways and Means,* 106th Cong. 2d sess. (October 6, 2000), p. 1363.

6. Neil Gilbert, "The Transformation of Social Services," *Social Services Review*, vol. 51, no. 4 (December 1977), pp. 624–41.

7. Atul Dighe, "Demographic and Technological Imperatives," in Lester M. Salamon, ed., *The State of Nonprofit America* (Brookings, 2002), p. 506.

8. Paul Ray and Sherry Ruth Anderson, *Cultural Creatives: How 50 Million People Are Changing the World* (San Francisco: Harmony Press, 2000); Dighe, "Demographic and Technological Imperatives," pp. 512–13.

9. Robert Avery and Michael Rendell, "Estimating the Size and Distribution of the Baby Boomers' Prospective Inheritances," Cornell University, Department of Consumer Economics, 1990. For more recent estimates, see John J. Havens and Paul G. Schervish, "Millionaires and the Millennium: New Estimates of the Forthcoming Wealth Transfer and the Prospects for a Golden Age of Philanthropy," Boston College, Social Welfare Research Institute, October 1999.

10. Edwin N. Wolff, *Top Heavy* (New York: New Press, 1995), table A-1. For a summary of the thinking on this intergenerational wealth transfer, see Harvey D. Shapiro, "The Coming Inheritance Bonanza," *Institutional Investor*, vol. 38, no. 6 (June 1994), pp. 143–48.

11. Steven Lawrence, Robin Gluck, and Dia Ganguly, *Foundation Yearbook, 2001* (New York: Foundation Center, 2000), p. 43.

12. Craig Smith, "The New Corporate Philanthropy," *Harvard Business Review* (May/June 1994), p. 107; Jane Nelson, *Business as Partners in Development: Creating Wealth for Countries, Companies, and Communities* (London: Prince of Wales Business Leaders Forum, 1996); Reynold Levy, *Give and Take: A Candid Account of Corporate Philanthropy* (Harvard Business School Press, 1999).

13. As third way theorist Anthony Giddens has put it: "The fostering of an active civil society is a basic part of the politics of the third way." Anthony Giddens, *The Third Way: The Renewal of Social Democracy* (Cambridge, U.K.: Polity Press, 1998), p. 78; David Osborne and Ted Gaebler, *Reinventing Government* (Reading, Mass.: Addison-Wesley Publishing, 1992).

14. The number of natural disasters tripled between the 1960s and the 1990s, while the number of armed conflicts, many of them civil wars, jumped from an average of 23 per year in the 1960s to over 40 per year in the 1990s. Shepard Forman and Abby Stoddard, "International Assistance," in Salamon, *The State of Nonprofit America*, p. 243.

15. Robert Putnam, *Bowling Alone: The Collapse and Revival of American Community* (Simon and Schuster, 2000).

16. *Social Security Bulletin, Annual Statistical Supplement* (2000), pp. 119–22.

17. House Committee on Ways and Means, *2000 Green Book*, p. 214. Expenditures are adjusted for inflation and expressed in 1999 dollars.

18. House Committee on Ways and Means, *2000 Green Book*, pp. 892–93; Teresa A. Coughlin, Leighton Ku, and John Holahan, *Medicaid since 1980: Costs, Coverage and the Shifting Alliance between the Federal Government and the States* (Washington: Urban Institute Press, 1994), p. 2; Steven Rathgeb Smith, "Social Services," in Salamon, *The State of Nonprofit America*, p. 162.

19. House Committee on Ways and Means, *2000 Green Book*, pp. 924, 927.

20. House Committee on Ways and Means, *2000 Green Book*, pp. 597, 953–54; Smith, "Social Services," p. 163.

21. Margaret J. Wyszomirski, "Arts and Culture," in Salamon, *The State of Nonprofit America,* pp. 189–90.

22. Coughlin, Ku, and Holahan, *Medicaid since 1980*, p. 87. For further detail, see Smith, "Social Services," p. 162.

23. House Committee on Ways and Means, *2000 Green Book*, p. 901.

24. House Committee on Ways and Means, *2000 Green Book*, p. 927.

25. Computed from data in *Social Security Bulletin*, 1997 and 1990.

26. House Committee on Ways and Means, *2000 Green Book*, p. 354.

27. The number of people on "welfare" fell by one-half between 1994 and 1999, from 14.2 million in 1994 to 7.2 million in 1999. In addition, the portion of those remaining on the rolls requiring full cash grants also declined, because more of them were working. Since states were guaranteed federal grants under the new Temporary Assistance for Needy Families (TANF) program at their peak levels of the early 1990s, and were also obligated to maintain their own spending on needy families at 75 percent of their previous levels, this meant significant resources were available for other purposes. House Committee on Ways and Means, *2000 Green Book,* pp. 376, 411.

28. For a general discussion of these "alternative tools" of public action, see Lester M. Salamon, "The New Governance and the Tools of Public Action: An Introduction," in Salamon, ed., *The Tools of Government: A Guide to the New Governance* (Oxford University Press, 2002), pp. 1–47. For a discussion of tax expenditures and loan guarantees, see Christopher Howard, "Tax Expenditures," in Salamon, *The Tools of Government*, pp. 410–44; and Thomas H. Stanton, "Loans and Loan Guarantees," in Salamon, *The Tools of Government*, pp. 381–409.

29. The $3.56 billion in subsidies made available to middle-income and lower-middle-income families through the day care tax credit thus exceeds the roughly $3 billion in subsidies provided to poor families through the Child Care and Development Block Grant.

Chapter 5

1. Rosabeth Moss Kanter and David V. Summers, "Doing Well while Doing Good: Dilemmas of Performance Management in Nonprofit Organizations and the Need for a Multiple-Constituency Approach," in Walter W. Powell, ed., *The Nonprofit Sector: A Research Handbook* (Yale University Press, 1987), p. 154.

2. Regina Herzlinger, "Can Public Trust in Nonprofits and Governments Be Restored?" *Harvard Business Review* (March/April 1996), p. 98.

3. Data assembled by Independent Sector, the national umbrella organization representing the nonprofit sector, suggest a considerable slowing of the rate of revenue growth for most components of the nonprofit sector during the most recent (1992–97) period. However, data generated from Form 990s filed by nonprofit organizations fail to confirm this slowdown. Thus, for example, while the Independent Sector data indicate real, inflation-adjusted

growth rates of 2.7 percent, 1.8 percent, and 3.8 percent per year for all non-profit organizations, for health organizations, and for social service organizations, respectively, during 1992–97, the Form 990 data show real increases of 4.4 percent, 2.9 percent, and 7.2 percent per year—nearly twice as great—for similar classes of organizations during virtually the same period, 1992–98. See Murray S. Weitzman and others, *The New Nonprofit Almanac and Desk Reference* (San Francisco: Jossey-Bass, 2002), pp. 102–03, 144–45.

4. U.S. Internal Revenue Service, *Data Book*, various years. Weitzman and others, *The New Nonprofit Almanac*, pp. 4–5. Nonprofit organizations are not required to incorporate or register with the Internal Revenue Service unless they have annual gross receipts of $5,000 or more and wish to avail themselves of the charitable tax exemption. Religious congregations are not required to register even if they exceed these limits, though many do register. It is therefore likely that more organizations exist than are captured in IRS records. It is also possible, however, that some of the new registrants are organizations that have long existed but have chosen to register only in recent years. Because the legal and financial advantages of registration are substantial, however, it seems likely that the data reported here represent real growth in the number of organizations, despite these caveats.

5. This same picture of organizational vitality emerges as well from detailed scrutiny of the Form 990s that registered nonprofit organizations are obliged to file with the Internal Revenue Service. Because these forms are only required of organizations with $25,000 or more in revenue, it might be assumed that older and larger organizations would dominate the reporting agencies. Yet, a recent analysis of these reporting organizations reveals that most of those in existence as of 1998 had been founded since 1985, and half of these had been founded since 1992. Weitzman and others, *The New Nonprofit Almanac*, p. 129.

6. Mark Chaves, "Religious Congregations," in Lester M. Salamon, ed., *The State of Nonprofit America* (Brookings, 2002), p. 284.

7. Julian Wolpert, *Patterns of Generosity in America: Who's Holding the Safety Net?* (New York: Twentieth Century Fund Press, 1993), pp. 7, 27, 39–40; Sarah Dewees and Lester M. Salamon, "Maryland Nonprofit Employment: 1999," Johns Hopkins Nonprofit Employment Bulletin no. 3 (May 2001).

8. Avis Vidal, "Housing and Community Development," in Salamon, *The State of Nonprofit America*, pp. 224, 228.

9. See, for example, Raymond Hernandez, "A Broad Alliance Tries to Head Off Cuts in Medicare," *New York Times*, May 13, 2001, p. Al.

10. Computed from data in Weitzman and others, *The New Nonprofit Almanac*, pp. 136, 168.

11. See, for example, Amy Goldstein, "States' Budget Woes Fuel Medicaid Cuts," *Washington Post,* October 11, 2002, p. A1; Timothy Egan, "A Prescription Plan Hailed as a Model Is a Budget Casualty," *New York Times,* March 6, 2003, p. A31.

12. Jonathan Cohn, "How Medicaid Was Set Adrift," *New York Times,* March 6, 2003, p. A31.

13. Virginia A. Hodgkinson , with Kathryn E. Nelson and Edward D. Sivak Jr., "Individual Giving and Volunteering," in Salamon, *The State of Nonprofit America,* p. 397.

14. Hodgkinson, "Individual Giving and Volunteering," p. 389.

15. In one of the special ironies of the nonprofit field, the principal generator of data on private charitable giving in the United States has long been the trade association representing the nation's leading *for-profit* fundraising firms, the American Association of Fund-Raising Counsel, Inc.

16. Harvey Lipman, "Survey Finds Rapid Rise in Assets and Grants of Donor-Advised Funds," *Chronicle of Philanthropy,* May 31, 2001, p. 10.

17. Leslie Lenkowsky, "Institutional Philanthropy," in Salamon, *The State of Nonprofit America,* pp. 373–74.

18. See, for example, Thomas J. Billitteri, "A Run for the Money: Growth in Donor-Advised Accounts Spurs Fierce Competition for Funds," *Chronicle of Philanthropy,* April 20, 2000, p. 1.

19. Chaves, "Religious Congregations," pp. 280, 283.

20. See, for example, William Diaz, "For Whom and for What? The Contributions of the Nonprofit Sector," in Salamon, *The State of Nonprofit America,* pp. 517–36.

21. AAFRC Trust for Philanthropy, *Giving USA 2002* (Indianapolis, 2002); "The Tide Turns: Donations to Big Charities Lag in Uncertain Economic Climate," *Chronicle of Philanthropy,* October 31, 2002, p. 28; David Streitfeld, "Donations Dried Up with Tech Stocks," *Los Angeles Times,* October 13, 2002, p. 1; Robert Hughes, "As Funds Fade, Symphonies Cut Their Programs, Salaries," *Wall Street Journal,* October 9, 2002.

22. Harvey Lipman and Elizabeth Schwinn, "The Business of Charity: Nonprofit Groups Reap Billions in Tax-Free Income Annually," *Chronicle of Philanthropy,* October 18, 2001, p. 25.

23. Margret J. Wyzsomirsky, "Arts and Culture," in Salamon, *The State of Nonprofit America,* pp. 191–94.

24. See, for example, Mary Williams Wals, "Hospital Group's Link to Company Is Criticized," *New York Times,* April 27, 2002, p. B1; Walt Bogdanich, "Two Hospital Fundraising Groups Face Questions over Conflicts," *New York Times,* March 24, 2002, p. A1.

25. Dennis Young and Lester M. Salamon, "Commercialization and Social Ventures," in Salamon, *The State of Nonprofit America*, pp. 431–34.

26. The Roberts Enterprise Development Fund, *Social Purpose Enterprises and Venture Philanthropy in the New Millennium* (San Francisco, 1999); www.independentsector.org/pathfinder, a website created by the Pathfinder Project of Independent Sector and the University of Maryland

27. Kevin P. Kearns, *Private Sector Strategies for Social Sector Success: The Guide to Strategy and Planning for Public and Nonprofit Organizations* (San Francisco: Jossey-Bass, 2000), p. 25.

28. Paul Light, *Making Nonprofits Work: A Report on the Tides of Nonprofit Management Reform* (Brookings, 2000), p. 82.

29. Based on recent offerings from John Wiley and Sons' website, www.wiley.co.uk/products/subject/business/nonprofit/management.html.

30. Frances Hesselbein, "Foreword," in Peter Drucker, *The Drucker Foundation Self-Assessment Tool*, rev. ed. (San Francisco: Jossey-Bass, 1999), p. vi.

31. Elizabeth T. Boris and Jeff Krehely, "Civic Participation and Advocacy," in Salamon, *The State of Nonprofit America*, p. 311.

32. Bradford H. Gray and Mark Schlesinger, "Health," in Salamon, *The State of Nonprofit America*, p. 93.

33. See, for example, Walter W. Powell and Jason Owen-Smith, "Universities as Creators and Retailers of Intellectual Property," in Burton Weisbrod, ed., *To Profit or Not to Profit: The Commercial Transformation of the Nonprofit Sector* (Cambridge University Press, 1998), pp. 169–93.

34. Tracy Thompson, "Profit with Honor," *Washington Post Magazine*, December 19, 1999, pp. 7–22; Bill Shore, *Revolution of the Heart: A New Strategy for Creating Wealth and Meaningful Change* (New York: Riverhead Books, 1995).

35. Susan Gray and Holly Hall, "Cashing in on Charity's Good Name," *Chronicle of Philanthropy*, July 20, 1998, p. 26; *Cause Related Marketing* (San Francisco: Business for Social Responsibility Education Fund, 1999).

36. Eyal Press and Jennifer Washburn, "The Kept University," *Atlantic Monthly* (March 2000), p. 39–40.

37. Rosabeth Moss Kanter, "From Spare Change to Real Change: The Social Sector as Beta Site for Business Innovation," *Harvard Business Review*, vol. 77, no. 3 (May/June 1999), pp. 122–32.

38. Aspen Institute, Nonprofit Sector Strategy Group, "The Nonprofit Sector and Business: New Visions, New Opportunities, New Challenges" (Washington, 2001).

39. For further elaboration, see Alan J. Abramson and Rachel McCarthy, "Infrastructure Organizations," in Salamon, *The State of Nonprofit America*, pp. 331–54.

40. According to Hall, this "invention" was undertaken to protect the institution of the private foundation and other charitable institutions supported by wealthy individuals from an attack in the 1960s by populist reformers worried about the antidemocratic influence these institutions wielded over the national economy and national life. Peter Hall, *Inventing the Nonprofit Sector and Other Essays on Philanthropy, Voluntarism, and Nonprofit Organizations* (Johns Hopkins University Press, 1992), pp. 66–80.

41. Gray and Schlesinger, "Health," pp. 90–92.

42. See, for example, Kurt Eichenwald, "Columbia/HCA Fraud Case May Be Widened, U.S. Says," *New York Times,* February 14, 1998, p. B1; Kurt Eichenwald, "Key Executive at HealthSouth Admits to Fraud," *New York Times,* March 27, 2003, p. C1; Andrew Pollack, "Tenet to Sell or Shut Hospitals and Cut Jobs," *New York Times,* March 19, 2003, p. C3.

43. In the first six months of 2000, Moody's Investors Service downgraded the bonds of 121 nonprofit hospitals, affecting $24 billion in bonds. Reed Abelson, "Demand, but No Capital, at Nonprofit Hospitals," *New York Times,* June 12, 2002, p. B1.

44. Robert Putnam, *Bowling Alone: The Collapse and Revival of American Community* (Simon and Schuster, 2000).

45. Boris and Krehely, "Civic Participation and Advocacy," p. 304.

46. Jeffrey Berry, *The New Liberalism: The Rising Power of Citizen Groups* (Brookings, 1999).

47. Berry, *The New Liberalism,* p. 119.

48. See, for example, Margaret E. Keck and Kathryn Sikkink, *Activists beyond Borders: Advocacy Networks in International Politics* (Cornell University Press, 1999); Anne M. Florini, ed., *The Third Force: The Rise of Transnational Civil Society* (Washington: Japan Center for International Exchange and Carnegie Endowment for International Peace, 2000).

49. Boris and Krehely, "Civic Participation and Advocacy," pp. 314–20.

50. Berry, *The New Liberalism,* pp. 119–52.

Chapter 6

1. Bradford H. Gray and Mark Schlesinger, "Health," in Lester M. Salamon, ed., *The State of Nonprofit America* (Brookings, 2002), pp. 72, 74–75.

2. A classic statement of this tension, focusing on a much earlier period, can be found in David Rosner, *A Once Charitable Enterprise: Hospitals and Health Care in Brooklyn and New York, 1885–1915.* (Princeton University Press, 1982). For more recent analyses, see Regina Herzlinger and William S. Krasker, "Who Profits from Nonprofits?" *Harvard Business Review* (January/February 1987), pp. 93–106; David S. Salkever and Richard G. Frank,

"Health Services," in Charles T. Clotfelter, *Who Benefits from the Nonprofit Sector* (University of Chicago Press, 1992), pp. 24–54.

3. Eyal Press and Jennifer Washburn, "The Kept University," *Atlantic Monthly* (March 2000), pp. 39–40. See also Donald Stewart, Pearl Rock Kane, and Lisa Scruggs, "Education and Training," in Salamon, *The State of Nonprofit America,* pp. 115–18, 120–22.

4. Margaret J. Wyszomirski, "Arts and Culture," in Salamon, *The State of Nonprofit America,* pp. 192–93.

5. Estelle James, "Commercialism among Nonprofits: Objectives, Opportunities, and Constraints," in Burton Weisbrod, ed., *To Profit or Not to Profit: The Commercial Transformation of the Nonprofit Sector* (Cambridge University Press, 1998), p. 273. For the alternative theory, see Burton Weisbrod, "Modeling the Nonprofit Organization as a Multiproduct Firm: A Framework for Choice," in Weisbrod, ed., *To Profit or Not to Profit,* pp. 47–64.

6. Evelyn Brody, "Agents without Principals: The Economic Convergence of the Nonprofit and For-Profit Organizational Forms," *New York Law School Law Review,* vol. 40, no. 3 (1996), pp. 457–536. See also Evelyn Brody, "Accountability and Public Trust," in Salamon, *The State of Nonprofit America,* pp. 471–98.

7. William Diaz, "For Whom and For What?" in Salamon, *The State of Nonprofit America,* pp. 517–24.

8. James, "Commercialism among Nonprofits," p. 279.

9. Amelia Kohm, David La Piana, and Heather Gowdy, "Strategic Restructuring: Findings from a Study of Integrations and Alliances among Nonprofit Social Service and Cultural Organizations in the United States," Discussion Paper PS-24 (Chicago: Chapin Hall Center for Children, 2000).

10. Gray and Schlesinger, "Health," p. 95.

11. Paul Light, "The Content of Their Character: The State of the Nonprofit Workforce," *Nonprofit Quarterly* (Fall 2002), p. 9.

12. "Please, Allow Us to Introduce Ourselves," *Nonprofit Quarterly* (Summer 2001), p. 3.

13. "Please, Allow Us to Introduce Ourselves," *Nonprofit Quarterly* (Summer 2001), p. 3 (quoting a Rolling Stones 1968 refrain).

14. Alan J. Abramson and Rachel McCarthy, "Infrastructure Organizations," in Salamon, *The State of Nonprofit America,* pp. 350–51.

15. Gray and Schlesinger, "Health," pp. 97–98.

16. Shepard Forman and Abby Stoddard, "International Assistance," in Salamon, *The State of Nonprofit America,* pp. 260–63.

17. Milt Freudenheim, "Quality Goals in Incentives for Hospitals," *New York Times,* June 24, 2002, p. C1.

18. Included here are the numerous reductions in income tax rates over the past two decades and the phasing out of the inheritance tax. See Virginia A. Hodgkinson, with Kathryn E. Nelson and Edward D. Sivak Jr., "Individual Giving and Volunteering," in Salamon, *The State of Nonprofit America*, pp. 401–03.

19. Under the existing tax deduction system, taxpayers are allowed to subtract their charitable contributions from their taxable income if they itemize their deductions. Since higher-income taxpayers face higher tax rates, however, the resulting deductions are "worth" more to them than to lower-income taxpayers or those who do not itemize their deductions. Tax credits, however, are deducted from the actual taxes a taxpayer owes. Credits can be set equal to the contribution or at some fraction of the contribution (for example, 40 percent of the contribution could be deducted from the tax bill).

Index